YEAR of the PLAGUE JOURNAL

Pandemic and Politics

March 2020 - March 2021

Anna Henny Dabney

Published by
Penny Henny Publishing

First published by Penny Henny Press
May 2021

ISBN: 978-0-9895993-9-9

Library of Congress Control Number:

2021937550

Printed in the United States of America

DEDICATION

In memory of Victor Albert Royer. I would never have thought of writing sonnets without his inspiration and encouragement.

INTRODUCTION

I didn't plan to publish a book. I simply wanted to leave a vivid account of COVID-19 for my young grandchildren. They were ages 7 and 10 when the pandemic swiftly swept across the globe in early 2020. William and Mia are living through these difficult times, but they are, for the most part, protected from the harsh realities of the lethal disease. COVID actually infected several younger family members as the year wore on. Luckily, their cases were relatively mild and had no lasting complications.

Since March 2020, my grandkids have been enrolled in remote learning. Their mother, a high school principal, works from the school site daily, spending long days in Zoom meetings while students and teachers remain online. Their father, a professional photographer, supervises their schoolwork. He has a terrific sense of humor and can be credited with keeping their spirits high during isolation. The young Lieras children get together now and then with their first cousins, wearing masks and distancing. The two families are thought to be a safe "pod."

Why did I decide to document COVID-19 for others as well? First, I worked in healthcare from 1983-2007. I was then, and still am, passionately interested in wellness and disease. In my community relations work, I wrote newsletters, brochure copy, press releases, and annual report descriptions of hospital programs and services. My writing was geared to the medical staff, employees, community outreach, and potential foundation donors. As director of public relations at two different hospitals, I planned and executed health fairs, held press conferences, and facilitated free community talks on current health-care topics.

Anna Henny Dabney worked for Mt. Diablo Medical Center in various capacities for over a decade.

For the Mt. Diablo Hospital Foundation's Community Speaker Series, I contacted and secured the participation of nationally known doctors and psychologists for our videotaped talks. Most were highly regarded physicians, public speakers and authors such as Carl Simonton, M.D., and Susan Love, M.D., with expertise in cancer prevention and treatment. Among other presenters were Dr. Wayne Dyer, an American self-help and spiritual author and motivational speaker, and Joan Borysenko, Ph.D., a leading expert on stress, spirituality, and the mind/body connection. After the videotaping, I assisted with the script. Health care remains a subject of intense interest to me.

A second reason for documenting COVID-19 was my recent awareness that the 100+ year pandemic had been anticipated. The 1918 Spanish Flu could have killed one or both of my future parents, who were 18 and 31 when the gruesome and highly contagious coronavirus hit with a fury. *I never heard my parents mention it in their lifetime.* My father was in Eastern France serving with the U.S. Army in latter phases of World War I. My beautiful mother had recently graduated from high school in San Antonio. Both of those areas were devastated by the virus. I decided to record for posterity this deadly pestilence taking such a toll on our society and globally.

Initially, I began writing only about the pandemic using the Shakespearean sonnet format. I called my project *Sonnets in the Time of COVID-19*. The discipline in covering a subject using only fourteen lines would be a good workout for my brain. It was also an excellent vehicle for expressing strong emotion, while rhyming schemes and vocabulary choices would also be a stretch.

For those early poems, I generally succeeded in using iambic pentameter, but as I broadened the subject matter to include environmental issues and politics, I was less successful in that demanding format. I began to use a *modified* sonnet format, maintaining the fourteen lines (three quatrains and a couplet), with ten or eleven syllables per line. Rhymes either alternated lines or were used in couplets. I have always liked to write rhyming poems, although most poets today write in free verse.

Since the beginning of Trump's presidency, I had written protest poems for Open Mic. I decided to try a modified sonnet format for those poems as well. The pandemic, global warming and governmental affairs are all interrelated, so it made sense to integrate all of them into my sonnet collection. Jean Gregory, a friend from my writers' group, suggested a term for my political sonnets that resonated – **poetic news flashes**. My end notes provided additional information that I didn't have the scope to cover in a fourteen-line poem. A busy person, Jean told me she looked forward to poems containing "breaking news" updates.

Immediately after Donald Trump was elected in 2016, I was consumed with a strong desire to work toward preserving our democracy. In my seventies, I thought it unsafe for me to march in protests. Instead, I joined a local chapter of *Indivisible.* The name of the chapter was "Nothing Rhymes with Orange."

As a member of *Indivisible*, I worked on environmental issues and registering older teens to vote. I also wrote postcards to voters in swing states, encouraging them to turn out to the polls. With my newfound zeal as a citizen, I became proactive in approaching key governmental officials by email, letters, and phone calls to register my opinions on important issues.

For me, expressing my feelings through writing poems became an effective way to deal with the stress and isolation imposed by prolonged sheltering in place. I also needed a constructive way to express my anger and frustration over Trump's disastrous policies affecting our environment, international relations, the rights of minorities, immigration, and the threats he posed to democracy itself. His mismanagement of the pandemic and his callous disregard for lives exposed to or lost to COVID-19 made me livid!

When Joseph R. Biden and Kamala Harris won the 2020 election, I was ecstatic! Hope was reborn in me, and my sleep patterns greatly improved. Just hearing Joe Biden, Ron Klain or Kamala Harris speak calmed me. The election ushered in the return of decency, competence, intelligence, good judgment, empathy, and compassion for others.

Our democracy has been tested under great stress, but it isn't down for the count yet. I will continue to exercise my citizenship responsibilities. We can NEVER become complacent.

CONTENTS

PART I - PANDEMIC AND POLITICS POEMS

PART II - NEVER TRULY GONE

PART III - Appendix

PART I – PANDEMIC AND POLITICS POEMS

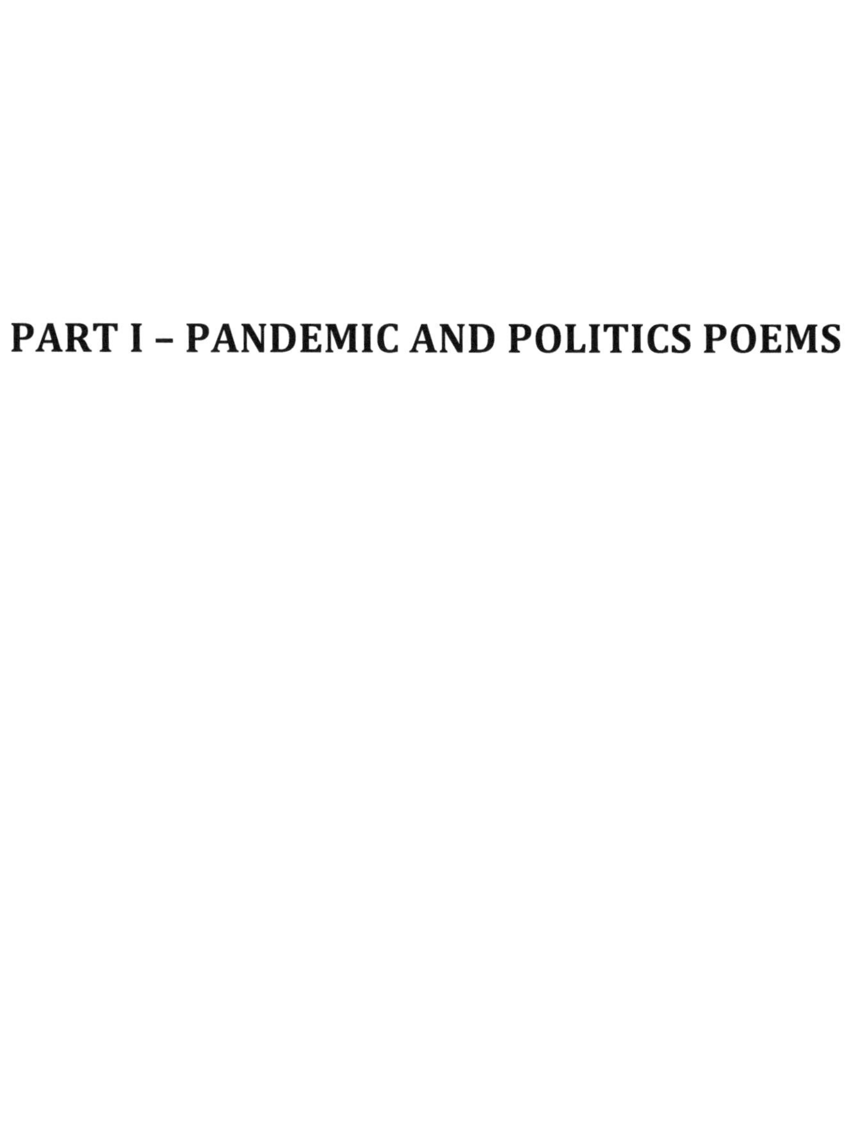

CORONAVIRUS LAMENT

Oh, I am weary of this troubled life,
Yet worried that each week may be my last.
Our president persists in causing strife.
How can I not be anxious and downcast?
The pestilence I'd dreaded has appeared;
Around the globe it multiplies each day.
Our valiant health care workers, *as we feared*,
Without the right protections pass away.
Without my darling, I am here alone,
Cut off from family and my dear friends,
Yet still in touch by email and by phone.
I wonder when this lethal virus ends.
    I pray to God my family be spared
    And all those in my life for whom I've cared.

3/29/2020

I was first made aware of the 1918 Spanish Flu in a chilling article published in *Smithsonian Magazine* in 2018.

My beloved partner Victor died four years ago of cancer. Except for short drives to keep my car battery charged, I remain at home alone. I am in a high-risk category due to my age.

In the beginning of the COVID-19 pandemic, we knew so little about transmission or lethality. I didn't know how to get food and other items needed. There was massive stockpiling of bottled water, toilet paper, paper towels, facial tissues, and fresh eggs were hard to find. People had no protective masks, Clorox wipes, gloves or hand sanitizer, and no vaccines had been developed to combat the novel coronavirus.

(Donald Trump served one term: January 2017 - January 20, 2021)

COVID-19 HEARTBREAK

As deaths approach the toll of Vietnam,
Blue Angels fly formations in clear skies
To pay dramatic tribute and to calm
The fears of those who dread a harsh demise:
To die without a family member there,
Instead, to say profound good-byes by phone;
No funerals concluded with a prayer
And unclaimed bodies with no earthly home.
The stress on healthcare workers is severe.
They isolate from husband or from wife
Afraid to pass on virus to those dear,
And, Dr. Breen today took her own life.
  When will this angst and agony be done?
  This universal battle at last won?

4/28/2020

Today, the number of persons confirmed with COVID-19 in the U.S. passed the one million mark. The death toll of over 58,000 rose above the number of U.S. service personnel killed in Vietnam.

Dr. Lorna Breen was a 49-year-old ER physician in New York who had recovered from COVID-19 recently. While visiting at her sister's home, she took her own life in despair.

"She put her life on the line to care for other people," said her father, Dr. Philip Breen. "She was in the trenches, so to speak, in the front lines as people were dying left and right around her." He said his daughter contracted the virus and stayed home for only a week. It was not enough time.

EARTH'S REBIRTH

The Earth shows us the error of our ways.
Our skies are blue, not filled with choking haze.
The ozone layer hole has been repaired.
Wild creatures venture forth that had not dared.
Astounding vistas lost can now be seen.
The hills and valleys once more are serene.
Canals in Venice are restored to clear,
And aircraft overhead we rarely hear.
How rapidly did Nature make her case!
The gift of "Eden" we must not deface.
Mankind must reinvent the way we live,
Or Nature may refuse one day to give.
   Let's heed the lessons of our mother Earth.
   Give thanks to God and celebrate her worth!

5/2/2020

COVID-19 rapidly encircled the globe, causing many nations to drastically cut back on business and social interactions. While it lasted, Earth showed signs of revitalization, and air quality greatly improved.

GEORGE PERRY FLOYD REMEMBERED

The name George Floyd is heard around the world.
His tragic murder triggered large-scale protests
Where mostly peaceful crowds braved tear gas hurled,
Police in riot gear and kevlar vests.
While lying face-down, handcuffed, on the ground
George pleaded "I can't breathe" repeatedly.
Eight minutes later, George could make no sound.
The officer refused to raise his knee.
This brutal Floyd arrest was captured boldly,
Shot bravely on a teenaged girl's cellphone.
The officer continued to stare coldly.
Without this video, would we have known?
  The legacy of George Floyd will shine bright.
  His death advanced the *Black Lives Matter* fight.

6/11/2020

In his eloquent and emotional testimony before a Congressional committee, George Floyd's brother Philonise Floyd asked, **"What is a Black man's life worth? Twenty dollars?"**

Officer Derek Chauvin, with 20 years of service on the Minneapolis Police Force, kept the full force of his knee on the neck of George Floyd for 8 minutes and 46 seconds, cutting off blood and oxygen to his brain. George Floyd's "infraction," trying to use a $20 bill suspected of being counterfeit to buy cigarettes. He may not even have known it was a a counterfeit bill.

DARE TO HOPE

My heart is beating with new hope today
That racial justice may not be a dream
Which, unachieved, will shortly fade away
As protest ends, with "rule of law" supreme.
These peaceful movements show a different face
From those of more than fifty years ago.
We witness young and old of varied race
Who come together in a common show.
They brave the tear gas and projectiles shot
While COVID plague surrounds them in the air.
They take a knee or lie prostrate, though hot.
May God protect them with the masks they wear.
    Small bands of looters strike when dark descends,
    But others intervene to see it ends.

6/3/2020

All four officers from the Minneapolis police force have been charged with murder in the death of 46-year-old George Floyd. Charges on Derek Chauvin, the main perpetrator, were raised from murder 3 to murder 2.

Some peaceful protesters tried to discourage looting or tagging of buildings from taking place. After dark, saboteurs and rioters moved in to strike as they looted, tagged buildings and set fires. As is usually the case, their actions made the idealistic marches of daytime protestors look bad.

THE ANGEL OF DEATH

When I have lived beyond my useful days,
And should Death's angel knock upon my door,
I would not stand there gaping, in a daze,
Or cry and plead with him to grant me more.
I'll raise my hand and say, "Come on inside.
Take comfort in my space while I prepare."
When death approaches with no place to hide,
One cannot turn away his icy glare.
"Lead on, dear angel, to a better home,"
I'd tell him after saying final prayers.
"For years I've trudged my thorn-laced path alone.
Together, we will mount the heav'nly stairs."
  My life on earth has been a blessed one.
  With joy, I'll know my vexing tasks are done.

6/7/2020

In the time of COVID-19, it is wise for the elderly to put their affairs in order and make known their end-of-life choices by updating their Advance Directives with their medical plan and family members.

I do not want to live with pain and disability. I will leave the **ventilator option** for younger people who have a better chance of surviving that ICU experience – especially those who have a full life ahead of them and children to raise.

In this first version, Death is more like the Grim Reaper, rather than a friend, former acquaintance, or gentle guide to Heaven's pearly gates. I wrote a second version that appears next, after hearing my friend Debbie's account of her near-death experience.

THE BENIGN ANGEL OF DEATH

When I have lived beyond my **hardy** days,
And if Death's angel knocks upon my door,
I would not stand there gaping, in a daze,
Or cry and plead with him to grant me more.
If near-death tales I've heard from friends are true,
Then death is not a fate that we should fear.
A loving spirit wreathed in light will greet you.
The angel sent as guide is someone dear.
"Lead on, kind angel, to a better home,"
I'd tell him after saying final prayers.
"For years I've trudged my thorn-laced path alone.
Together, we will mount the Heav'nly stairs."
  My life on Earth has been a blessed one.
  With joy, I'll know my vexing tasks are done.

6/7/2020

This **second version** is for my dear friend Debbie, who experienced and described to me a powerful near-death experience that changed her life and greatly strengthened her faith. I include it as an alternate version to the preceding poem I wrote first, *The Angel of Death*. It is essentially the same poem with perhaps a more positive outlook.

LOSING IT

My mind is like a raging waterfall
That tumbles over boulders strewn below.
I struggle daily to keep track of all
The currents and to learn what I must know.
I find it hard to be old and alone
While also staring COVID in the face;
My contact with my children is by phone,
And, if together, we could not embrace.
The threats I see grow more severe each day
With news and civic mayhem stoking fear
While global warming hasn't gone away,
And wildfire season soon will reappear.
    My meditation apps are rarely used.
    My internet is lost; I am bemused.

6/15/2020

At this stage of the COVID-19 pandemic, we did not yet have ZOOM sessions available to keep families scattered across the nation connected. Having that resource for me months later has made all the difference. I can keep up with my grandchildren's progress in virtual learning and observe how rapidly they are growing and transforming.

Unfortunately, my internet was frequently out of service for two months while my cable provider repaired and upgraded their underground cables on my street.

GRATITUDE

What cause have I to feel sad or lament?
Compared to some, I'm in a favored space.
I have supplies and food that I need sent
So I don't have to venture from my place.
I've reached the age to pace myself ... retired.
Each day I walk and write or watch TV.
I have no job where I risk being fired.
My writer friends each week reach out to me.
I'm glad to have a roof above my head,
With homelessness and hunger all around.
I've no young children that I must keep fed.
My bed is cozy, and my sleep is sound.
  I'm blessed with good health and my family.
  When COVID risk is gone, they'll visit me.

6/17/2020

I have not ventured into a grocery store since the "shelter in place" directive was issued in California last March. I rely on Instacart, or small produce markets that deliver, for my groceries and paper supplies. In the beginning, there were shortages of toilet paper, paper towels, Kleenex, and even eggs. It was a scary time, and I felt quite vulnerable.

I am in a high-risk group and I'm not taking any unnecessary risks. I walk almost daily for 25 minutes, always wearing a mask.

THE THINGS I MISS

What do I miss in a time such as this?
A body massage, a hug and a kiss.
Without the mask, warm greetings and a smile;
My hairdresser's magic. She knows my style.
My house sparkling clean in just a few hours;
A guest here for dinner who brings me flowers.
A walk with a friend while close to each other;
A visit in Oakland from my Texas brother.
Hearing live music in a concert hall;
Planning a trip to take place in the fall.
Singing old hymns in my church on Sundays;
Writers' group meetings and feedback on Mondays.
  One day we'll emerge from this harsh nightmare
  As we lay aside fear and *show* we care.

6/18/2020

P.S. I long for those family occasions
  When we all gathered and freely embraced.
  How many more of these celebrations
  Must we pass up 'til COVID is erased?

INSANITY

Large throngs of foolish folks and miscreants
Obey their leader's call, to their demise.
To hold large rallies indoors makes no sense;
To be there would be careless and unwise.
What kind of man subjects his faithful fans
To unsound actions with such consequence
As COVID ranges all around the stands?
They go despite the risks and evidence.
Within three weeks, long after they disband
To outposts scattered widely in our nation,
Will all those stricken come to understand
And as they die, pray hard for their salvation?
    The virulent virus spreads contagion
    To others absent on that occasion.

6/20/2020

Donald Trump insists that all those attending his June 20th political rally in Tulsa, Oklahoma sign waivers, acknowledging that they can't sue him if they become ill with COVID-19 after attending. There will be no social distancing inside the enclosed arena that holds 20,000, and people are actively discouraged from wearing face masks.

Former presidential candidate Herman Cain attended the packed rally in Tulsa. Shortly afterward, he and about seven Trump staffers tested positive for COVID-19. After battling the disease for a month, Cain died at age 74.

THE NEW NORMAL

Walking today with an eerie feeling,
Nothing seemed normal. My brain was reeling.
The mockingbirds' songs put me into a trance.
I kept my distance from a friend's advance.
Workers were making repairs to cables.
Van drivers dropped off food items and staples.
Young joggers and walkers sometimes breezed past.
I trudged up the hill, as I cannot walk fast.
How many days have I sheltered in place,
Longing to meet friends in groups, face to face?
One hundred fourteen – they all blur together –
With most hours indoors, despite good weather.
  I feel a detached unreality
  In a world that often bewilders me.

6/22/2020

Today, I walked for an hour, all the way up my steep street and back. I cross the street when a walker or jogger approaches on the same sidewalk, and I wear a mask. I'm grateful to live on a wide street in a beautiful neighborhood.

Comcast is still working on perplexing problems with their buried cable lines on my street, trying to replace and upgrade them. I typically have internet connectivity and cable TV for only six or seven hours in a 24-hour period. This additional stress adds to my sense of being cut off from life as usual.

I can't rely on being able to access Zoom for meetings, virtual medical appointments, or visits with my Southern California family. I shouldn't complain, as some have much more serious problems to deal with.

TRAITOR

The most disturbing news is in the air
That Trump has once more sold his soul to Putin.
"A hoax," he cries; "The charges are unfair."
His staff denies the facts they are disputing.
Our soldiers in Afghanistan are killed
By Taliban who earn a large amount
From Russia for each bloody contract filled.
For these vile deeds, they must be held to account.
We've been preoccupied by our pandemic,
Around the globe our cases "number one."
Coronavirus here is now endemic.
It seems a shift in focus has begun.
    We must rise up and oust this evil man.
    Turn out the vote, do everything we can!

7/1/2020

Taliban-inspired militants are revealed to have received a payment of up to $100,000 in Russian rubles for each American or coalition soldier killed. The autocratic President of Russia Vladimir Putin is thought to be behind the payment of bounties.

President Trump claims he was not informed of the bounties paid by Russia, or it wasn't considered an "actionable or credible threat." Numerous reputable sources say information was included in Trump's Presidential Daily Briefings in February of 2020, and possibly even a year earlier. Some sources say Trump was given a verbal briefing by his staff and a list of recommended options to respond to Putin's aggression. Trump never did anything to stem the threat or confront Putin in any way. Rather than impose punitive measures on Putin, he decided to withdraw over 8,000 American troops from Germany, and he advocates re-admitting Russia into the G-7 coalition of European countries.

THE COVID THREAT

Your name resounds around me every day.
You are unwelcome here. Go on your way.
You answer by increasing stealth and pace.
I feel your fetid breath upon my face.
Your bony fingers glide across my skin,
I fear that you will find your way within.
I bolt my doors and try to block your entry
And pray my watchful angels will stand sentry.
I sanitize until my hands are red.
Each night, I gladly slip into my bed.
I read of new contagion and feel weepy.
I calm myself with music 'til I'm sleepy.
  One day we'll find a way to conquer you.
  'Til then, I'll follow what we're told to do.

7/2/2020

*Don't touch your face
*Wear a mask around others
*Keep social distancing of 6 -10 feet
*Wash hands frequently with the right technique
*Avoid large groups
*For "at risk" populations, stay home unless absolutely necessary to go out, except for exercise.
*Sanitize surfaces others may have touched

On this day, there are 2,704,017 confirmed COVID-19 cases in the U.S. New cases are surging by 56,000 daily. Over 128,000 have died in our country. New cases are skyrocketing, especially in states such as Arizona where Trump recently held huge indoor campaign rallies where most were not wearing masks. Testing and contact tracing is still inadequate. We have more COVID cases here than in any other country. Europe banned U.S. citizens from traveling there.

A SURREAL FOURTH OF JULY

Our July Fourth is quite surreal this year,
A patchwork quilt of fetes across the nation.
The strangest, at Mount Rushmore, evokes fear
Of virus spread and risk of conflagration.
Trump chose this spot to greet his loyal base
With firework shows where risk of fire is high.
Carved presidents will glower from the cliff face
While rockets are exploding in the sky.
The South Dakota governor declared
No masks or distancing will be required.
Sioux tribal leaders protest, to be spared
The risk to them of pestilence and fire.
    As always, Trump is focused on "the show,"
    Wreaking havoc wherever he may go.

7/3/2020

The Black Hills of South Dakota are sacred to the Sioux Indians. In the 1868 treaty, signed at Fort Laramie and other posts in Sioux country, the U.S. recognized the Black Hills as part of the Great Sioux Reservation, set aside for exclusive use by the Sioux people. In 1874, however, General George Custer led an expedition into the Black Hills, accompanied by miners who were seeking gold. Once gold was found there, miners soon moved into the Sioux hunting grounds and demanded protection from the U.S. Army. Soon, the Army was ordered to confront wandering bands of Sioux who were hunting on the range in accordance with treaty rights. In 1876, Custer, leading an Army detachment, encountered the encampment of Sioux and Cheyenne at the Little Bighorn River. Custer's detachment was annihilated. The United States would continue its battle against the Sioux in the Black Hills until the government confiscated the land in 1877. To this day, Black Hills ownership remains disputed.

WHITE NATIONALIST RALLY

Trump's campaign rallies had a racist tinge –
Juneteenth weekend, Tulsa and Mount Rushmore.
His speech's undertones caused me to cringe.
Now, plans for a "statue garden" are in store.
Trump praised the virtues of our nation's founders,
Though slave-holding pasts may tarnish some names.
He hopes to gloat if Biden's bid flounders.
His team will resort to political games.
He's wrapped himself up in our nation's flag,
While praising past presidents we admired,
As though he also has reason to brag.
I say to voters, "Let's tell him, 'You're fired!'"
    Would any president preceding him
    Endanger his base for a selfish whim?

7/4/2020

The four presidents with portraits carved into Mt. Rushmore are: Washington, Jefferson, (Teddy) Roosevelt, and Lincoln.

Holding a rally with 7,500 people, such as the one held at the foot of Mt. Rushmore, while COVID-19 is out of control in the U.S., is the height of irresponsibility. There was no social distancing, hardly a mask was seen, and people were shouting and cheering – behaviors known to widely disperse tiny droplets of contagion into the air. In addition, massive fireworks launched from above the cliff face could have set off a forest fire. Chemical residues are known to damage the environment, especially groundwater. Native American tribes, who rightfully claim that land and decry the "desecration" of their sacred mountain, are furious about the event held there on July 3rd.

Trump's long-running TV show *The Apprentice* featured him as a CEO whose signature move was to declare, "You're fired!"

AGORAPHOBIA

Agoraphobia is a Greek word:
Fear to venture into the marketplace.
After five months at home, it seems absurd
That I might *reluctantly* leave my space.
When a COVID vaccine at last is here,
I will eagerly show up to get mine,
After routine masks and pervasive fear
Of places enclosed and standing in line.
How will I cope with close contact again?
Massages, pedicures and hairstyling,
Dentists, or indoor dining with a friend?
Getting through airports and once more flying?
    Am I becoming too fond of my home
    And even enjoying my time alone?

7/7/2020

I began sheltering in place around mid-February of 2020. It seems I become more comfortable with my self-imposed quarantine every month.

I write, walk almost daily, watch news, read, enjoy movies and listen to classical music. Our writers' group twice a month continues to meet with Zoom, and we are hosting virtual Open Mic performances. Talking with friends and family by phone helps a great deal also. When I walk with my mask on, I often have conversations with neighbors who have lived here for decades, as I have.

THE EDUCATION CATASTROPHE

I'm fretting for the children of this land
Who may return to education soon.
We must first get this pestilence in hand,
With complex plans that public schools fine-tune.
I understand what parents must endure.
How can they work if young kids learn from home?
But, uppermost in mind, they must ensure
The safety of their children, and their own.
This plague is wrecking our society
In countless ways we've never seen before.
The stress can trigger loss of one's sobriety –
With layoffs, hunger, homelessness and more.
  Our nation could have known a kinder fate
  If those in charge had not responded late.

7/13/2020

Trump threatened to pull federal funding from schools that fail to open. Secretary of Education Betsy DeVos echoed those empty threats. They have no PLANS to safely open schools in the fall. Trump is focused mainly on the economy and stock market indexes and their relevance to his re-election prospects. Highest risks are to school administrators, teachers, support staff, cafeteria workers, custodians, and school bus drivers. Young children can carry the COVID infection home and cause severe illness or death to family members – especially in multi-generational households. My daughter is a high school principal in Anaheim, California, where most schools are conducting virtual learning.

Trump unleashed wrath on top expert in disease and epidemiology, Dr. Anthony Fauci. Trump banned him from his advisory capacity to the White House and press briefings. Dr. Fauci worked successfully with five previous presidents and he is respected internationally.

THE CONSCIENCE OF THE HOUSE HAS DEPARTED

John Lewis' death was announced today.
He and I were the same age of eighty.
We both grew up in the southern USA,
But the obstacles *he* faced were weighty.
I recall Black folks treated like *the other*.
A *"colored"* water fountain had me confused.
I drank and was rebuked by my mother.
I thought it would gush forth in rainbow hues.
John Lewis fought for justice all his life,
Enduring beatings and jail when needed.
His calm demeanor sought to minimize strife.
Persistence caused his words to be heeded.
    I embraced racial justice in my own way,
    When I chose to wed Bob – on my birthday.

7/17/2020

John Lewis died on July 17, 2020. The U.S. Representative, born in Alabama to sharecropper parents, served 17 terms (1986-2020) representing the 5th District in Georgia. He was beloved!

I was about six or seven when I read the "colored" sign on a water fountain and drank from it. Blacks lived on another side of town, and we rarely encountered them in the 1940s. I recall seeing separate restrooms and waiting areas in bus stations.

Bob and I eloped to be married by a justice of the peace. My birthday wedding took place after the end of the fall school semester. Another American teacher took my place after I resigned to move to Berlin with my husband.

STORMTROOPERS

The nightmare I most feared has me alarmed.
Trump's troops are snatching peaceful folks at will.
In camouflage and helmets, they are armed
With lethal weapons, bent on doing ill.
They wear no badges, spring from unmarked cars.
Protestors are not charged or read their rights.
The city's mayor has opposed this farce.
Some innocents are kept for several nights.
These outside agents had not been invited.
The local leaders had the scene in hand.
This bogus force must leave, or soon be cited.
A great outcry is heard throughout our land.
    Trump is implicated in this travesty,
    These covert actions pain the world to see.

7/18/2020

Portland, Oregon has had largely peaceful protests since the murder of George Floyd on **5/25/2020** by four Minneapolis policemen. One protestor, standing and holding a boom box, was shot in the head with a projectile. He suffered bleeding at the scene and was hospitalized for serious concussions. Any protestors being locked up may be exposed to COVID-19 while in jail.

Is Trump calling in these troops without consultations with local officials to detract from mismanagement of COVID-19 and to burnish his image as the "law and order" president? This display of force may be a dress rehearsal for trying to remain in office using force if he loses.

These thugs severely beat and tear-gassed a 53-year-old Naval Academy graduate and veteran who approached them asking who they were and who dispatched them. He took body blows until they sprayed his face.

BACK TO SCHOOL COVID BLUES

My heart is troubled for schoolchildren here
Who all across our land may fall behind;
And, worse, they live each day with COVID fear,
With safe activities so hard to find.
My grandkids will engage in distance learning.
They're fortunate to have their dad at home,
But online study can't efface their yearning
To be with friends and teachers – and to roam.
Will these strange times leave scarring that goes deep,
With children fearing closeness or infection?
Will they be anxious or have troubled sleep?
This early, these signs may escape detection.
  Most children can adjust and will survive,
  And, one day, without COVID, they will thrive.

8/3/2020

I worry whether my grandson Will, age eleven this month, and Mia, who turns eight in October, might harbor secret fears, as I have, that one or both of their parents might die of COVID-19. Their mother is a high school principal who goes in to work with staff, but she is taking precautions against this insidious infection.

I have decided to take on a special project to help my daughter's family. I will serve as my grandson's remote learning language arts tutor or coach. I plan to help him with his creative writing and interpretation of poems. I also want to nurture his innate interest in nature and wildlife. When Mia is older, I will work with her, too. My expertise as an educator for nine years involved teaching English skills to middle school students.

PANDEMIC PANDEMONIUM

Our pandemic is spreading like wildfire
Due to lack of serious compliance,
With no one in charge who can inspire
And so many displaying defiance.
Donald Trump tries to downplay the cases.
"It *is* what it *is*," he comments and shrugs,
Unmoved by all those the virus erases,
Or Dr. Fauci getting death threats from thugs.
Trump's focus is on his re-election,
Though his posturing and threats meet deaf ears
As his dictates to schools meet rejection.
Most parents will be guided by their fears.
    This lethal virus can be extinguished
    By choosing a *leader* who's distinguished.

8/6/2020

On this date over 164,000 Americans have died of COVID-19.

Dr. Anthony Fauci is our country's foremost and esteemed epidemiologist, highly respected internationally. He continues to speak truth to power. As a consequence, he and his family members now require special security to protect them!

Former Vice President Joseph Biden is the Democratic candidate for president. At this point, he is well ahead of Trump in the polls, but many political games are being played by the Trump administration. They are soliciting interference from foreign governments, disparaging mail-in voting as fraudulent, slowing the U.S. Mail, purging legitimate voters from databases, and reducing polling sites.

IDIOTIC BEHAVIOR

The news is often distressing to hear.
Thousands of bikers are holding a rally.
On Harleys, they will ride from far and near.
New COVID cases will be hard to tally.
These bikers will meet up in South Dakota,
Most with no spacing or masks on their faces.
Once more endangering local Lakota,
A tribe exposed in July in these spaces.
These rowdy folks will spread their contagion
In local hotels and cafes and bars.
No one would dare to issue a citation.
Returning home, they will trigger new horrors.
  Will they leave behind them a new *Trail of Tears*
  From the worst pandemic in one hundred years?

8/9/2020

Up to 250,000 bikers on Harley-Davidson motorcycles are expected in Sturgis, South Dakota over 10 days for their 80th Annual Rally. Local residents and a few bikers worry that crowds could create a "super-spreader" event. Most won't wear a mask or socially distance. Pure insanity and utter selfishness! I can't think of a better way to distribute COVID-19 more widely around our nation. The town imposes no limits on crowds indoors and has no mask mandates. The South Dakota governor is welcoming visitors for money they will spend.

On this date, over 162,000 persons in the U.S. have died of COVID-19. Estimates are that the death toll will rise to 300,000 by December 1, if things continue on the same trajectory. Over 5 million people in the U.S. have been diagnosed with COVID.

OH, HAPPY DAY!

I shout, “Oh frabjous day, callooh, callay!”
Kamala Harris was chosen today
To run on the ticket with Joseph Biden,
Whom Trump has accused of staying in hiding.
Residing in Oakland, I am so proud
That one of our own stands above the crowd
Of other women whom Biden vetted.
I know his choice will not be regretted.
This campaign will take on new energy
When together they show their synergy.
The voting begins on October third.
Let’s all vote early; make our voices heard.
    I feel new hope for the future today,
    That Donald Trump will be sent on his way!

8/11/2020

During this campaign season in the grips of COVID-19, Vice President Biden has wisely chosen to keep a low profile, socially distance, wear a mask, and campaign “virtually” instead of before large crowds like Donald Trump. He has been discreet and has successfully modeled what we all should be doing to halt the pandemic’s spread. Trump rarely even wears a mask. The president has held super-spreader political rallies and repeatedly tells lies about the marauding virus, saying it is “going away, is under control, and will soon disappear.” He also says that children are practically immune. *Facebook* removed that tweet due to his misrepresenting of vital health information.

I borrowed the opening words of joy from Lewis Carroll’s poem *The Jabberwocky*, one of my favorites.

THE FUTILITY OF FATALITIES

A new word was coined by Trump yesterday.
Twice he uttered the “word” *fatilities*.
I gathered what he was trying to say,
That he couldn’t pronounce *fatalities*.
Unaware that the new word he used made sense,
The deaths we are seeing are unneeded.
They’re futile, pointless ... there is no defense,
Avoidable if guidelines were heeded.
Biden and Harris are not holding back,
Directing withering criticism
At policies and planning which they lack,
Suggesting bold steps, not cynicism.
    How inspiring it was to see this team
    Daring to restore our American dream.

8/13/2020

Fatilities: the futility of COVID-19 fatalities!

MICHELLE OBAMA SPEAKS OUT

Michelle Obama was magnificent
In her headlining convention address.
Her message was profound and eloquent
With perspective only she could express.
Each word that she uttered was insightful,
Using simple words that held great power.
The outlook for our country appears frightful!
We must install new leadership to flower.
Our hopes for our democracy grow dim
Unless we rise up and we vote Trump out!
Many want officials to arrest him.
If that day comes, we'll celebrate and shout!
Thank you, Michelle, for your passionate voice.
This nation's future depends on our choice!

8/18/2020

Michelle Obama was our elegant First Lady for Obama's two terms in office (2009-2016). A graduate of Harvard Law School and Princeton University, she is an outstanding speaker. While in the White House, she ignored racial epithets, saying, "When they go low, we go high."

The First Lady developed projects to work with children in planting vegetable gardens, using a plot developed on the South Lawn. Food grown was used for the First Family's meals and sent to food banks. Their two young daughters, Sasha and Malia, grew up beautifully during their time in the White House.

In 2018, Michelle published her best-selling memoir, ***Becoming.*** In it, she talks about her roots and how she found her voice, as well as her time in the White House, her public health campaign, and her role as a mother. She is rated one of the most-admired women in the world.

BUILD BACK BETTER

I watched Joe Biden's speech *again* today,
Accepting our party's nomination.
Each time, I couldn't keep my tears away,
With hope that we can end Trump's domination.
Our country is in need of restoration,
A return to kindness and compassion;
An end to vestiges of segregation,
With MAGA hats completely out of fashion.
Joe Biden spoke with strength and clarity
Of how we can address this nation's woes
While standing up for workers' parity.
He promised not to coddle our main foes.
    I *know* that we selected the right man.
    We all must vote in any way we can.

8/21/2020

Joe Biden understands the tragedy of the uncontrolled spread of COVID-19 and that we must get this pestilence under control before our economy can come back. He expressed sympathy to families who have lost loved ones to this hideous plague. Biden and Harris and other Democrats at the Convention modeled mask-wearing and social distancing behavior. The U.S. under Joe Biden will gear up to produce plenty of PPE (personal protective equipment) in our own country.

At the successful *virtual* convention, Biden announced he intends to govern in the interest of ALL citizens, not just those who voted for him. He pledged to preserve Social Security and Medicare and expand health care. He has plans to revitalize our dilapidated infrastructure and to combat climate change.

EVACUATION COMPLICATIONS

I wait and pray my own home will be spared.
I parked my Camry pointed toward the street.
I packed my masks and Lysol wipes with care
And also healthy snacks that I can eat.
Evacuation is much harder now
With COVID lurking just behind the fires.
I don't know where to go or even how
To guard myself as the virus conspires.
It's hard to shelter safely with no shelter
And carry with me all the things I'd need
When life appears like crazy helter-skelter,
With many that we need to house and feed.
  These lightning fires are burning up our state.
  Could Mother Earth be saying we're too late?

8/22/2020

More dry lightning storms are expected for the next three days. It's impossible to anticipate where fires could ignite in areas such as mine with many stressed trees and lots of dry underbrush. This time of year is a nail-biter!

EVACUATION LAMENTATIONS

Preparing to evacuate is hard.
So many things I hate to leave behind.
My packed car I'd find difficult to guard,
And most things that I value, one of a kind.
I thank the Lord for being merciful,
Relieved we had no lightning strikes last night!
Air quality today, a bit more healthful,
And firemen may make headway in their fight.
I'm staying tuned to radio updates.
The red flag warning recently expired.
I think of refugees in wars whose fates
Were so much worse than what they had desired.
    I pray to God to spare our suffering state
    From trials such as we've gone through of late.

8/24/2020

Over 12,000 dry lightning strikes set massive fires across California, most in Northern California, last week. The terrifying electrical storms flashed and rumbled overhead every few seconds, lasting for over three hours. Little or no moisture accompanied them. As a result, our state is burning up, with over 600 major fires out of control. Red flag warnings are alerts issued when wind velocities are expected to reach between 60 and 90 miles per hour during our expanded "dry season."

Our firefighting resources are limited. In past wildfire seasons, large amounts of prison labor were used fighting fires. Prison populations have been reduced by 17,000 due to high risk of COVID-19 contagion in those groups. Back-up firefighting resources from other states have taken up to a week to arrive. In Livermore, California, in the Bay Area, air quality this week was termed "hazardous." Our air quality was the worst in the world.

THE TRUMP CONVENTION

This Convention was the strangest I've seen.
Melania spoke dressed in Army green.
The entire Trump family put on a show,
And there was young Barron; how fast he did grow!
The White House lawn set the stage for the event
With folks packed together by their consent.
How could they choose to endanger their health?
To cling to their jobs and maintain their wealth?
Trump sought to show an illusion of power
Over COVID, killing more by the hour.
He cared not at all for the others there,
With few wearing masks and chants in the air.
  The spectacle ended in sparking the night
  With the Trump last name emblazoned in light.

8/28/2020

Melania wore a double-breasted army green suit with a militaristic appearance. Was she subtly warning us of things to come or possibly endorsing the Trump campaign's focus on law and order?

Crowd size was estimated between 1,500 and 2,000 people seated next to one another for rows and rows. Trump's key staff members (several of them elderly) were seated on the front row, with no masks in evidence. Many droplets of contagion spewed forward from mouths of cheering and adoring crowds. Those behaviors are known to easily transmit COVID-19, even outdoors. Fireworks were blasted overhead at the conclusion of the event.

U.S. deaths from COVID-19 have risen to about 182,923 at latest count today, by far the largest number of fatalities than in any other country around the globe.

THE TRAGEDY OF JACOB BLAKE

The tale of Jacob Blake will long be told.
His actions to break up a fight were bold.
Two officers soon came upon the scene,
Not knowing how he'd tried to intervene.
Their case to place him under arrest was thin.
An officer's taser failed to subdue him.
Blake strode to his car with his three sons inside.
When viewers saw what happened next, they cried!
One officer held a gun to his back.
Blake opened the door and was under attack.
In front of his sons, he was shot seven times.
The bullets all lodged quite near to his spine.
  Now Blake is paralyzed from the waist down.
  People come to protest from miles around.

8/29/2020

On August 23, with three young sons in the back seat of his car, Jacob Blake was shot seven times point blank in his back by Kenosha, Wisconsin Police Officer Rusten Sheskey. He and two other officers were responding to a domestic abuse call. Blake had an outstanding warrant, and he resisted arrest.

Blake was taken to a Milwaukee hospital where he now lies paralyzed from the waist down – perhaps permanently. One leg was shackled to his hospital bed. After strong protests, the shackles were removed.

This shooting, captured on cell phone video, sparked vigorous outcries against racial injustice and police brutality. Nightly demonstrations have occurred since, attracting Antifa (anti-fascists) saboteurs and conservatives with AR-15 military style rifles.

SUCKERS AND LOSERS

The military vote may be the key
To winning by the Democrats this year.
In recent news reports, they clearly see
Trump's disrespect for fallen ones held dear.
"Losers" are those bravely lost in battle,
And "suckers" when they volunteered to serve.
He dodged the draft with "bone spurs;" no one tattled.
To go to war, he'd never have the nerve.
In France, he shirked his chance to honor war dead,
Concerned his hair would suffer in the rain.
He made up reasons not to drive ahead,*
The only head of state to act so vain.
  The emperor has no clothes, we can see.
  Will they vote for a Biden victory?

9/7/2020

The trip to the cemetery was only 40 miles by automobile from Paris. Trump is reported to have said to his aides, "Why should I go to that cemetery? It's filled with losers." Those fallen soldiers he referred to were 1,800 U.S. Marines slain at Belleau Wood in World War I.

NATURE'S WARNING

Mother Nature glowers above today.
Bright orange clouds like twilight are prevailing.
Vast wildfires spew thick smoke from miles away.
The message loud and clear, our earth is ailing.
Why don't we heed the threat of global warming
when scientists direct us to change course?
This crisis now at hand had ample warning.
Protections we have now Trump won't enforce!
Fine ash like snow is falling on our landscape.
Poor quality of air keeps us inside.
We must conserve and start to innovate,
Or soon discover there's no place to hide.
    Has our COVID focus weakened resolve
    To address climate issues we *must* solve?

9/9/2020

This bizarre day was surreal! The morning dawned with eerie skies glowing a bright red-orange that lingered for hours. The sun never once penetrated thick overcast in Oakland all day. Darkness at noon was like a total eclipse, only it lasted much longer. We understood the cause. Skies clogged with thick smoke from horrendous wildfires near us. Streetlamps stayed on all day. My backyard birds were disoriented, as were we humans. Fine ash fell like snowflakes and coated objects in the yard. Air outdoors was hazardous to breathe. I donned my N-95 mask if I had to go outdoors briefly. Everyone said it was *apocalyptic*, end times. Mother Nature gave us a strong message today – change your ways, or else!

HE KNEW!

He knew! Since February 7th, he knew
The dangers of COVID that he kept from you.
He stated on tape he sought to "downplay."
How lethal it was, he failed to portray.
He continued in speeches to deny,
While folks around us continued to die.
Trump *knew* COVID spread from droplets in air,
Yet hosted packed rallies taking no care.
He was protected on his lofty stage.
Unconcern for his fans fills me with rage!
How could he mistreat his base in this way?
A selfish narcissist on full display.
  Trump's main focus is on winning again.
  Disregard for life is a capital sin.

9/11/2020

Today is the 19th anniversary of attacks by al-Qaeda on the World Trade Center Twin Towers on September 11, 2001. Every three or four days, we are losing the equivalent of the 3,000 persons who died in the infamous 9-11 attacks. Over 192,000 have now died of COVID-19.

News sources tell us that Trump was warned by China on January 28, 2020, that COVID would be the biggest challenge of his presidency. On February 7, 2020, Trump was interviewed by eminent journalist and author Bob Woodward on this topic. He had been displeased with the way he was characterized in Woodward's first book about him, titled *RAGE*. He had declined to be interviewed for that book. Against advice he received, Trump agreed to be interviewed for Woodward's second book about his presidency. In taped interviews, the President revealed that he was aware early in 2020 how deadly COVID-19 was. Trump explained that he always tried to *downplay* the dangers, as he didn't want to cause panic.

A SHORT REPRIEVE

A reprieve from smoke is welcome today,
After long days of remaining inside.
The season of wildfire is here to stay
Until winter's rains have turned back the tide.
The act of walking outdoors with blue skies
Is a joy that can't be overstated.
But when Diablo winds materialize,
I may think California overrated.
On days like today, with a hint of fall,
I am grateful for my home and good health,
Yet I know I could quickly lose it all
From a wildfire that approaches with stealth!
  It's hard to live with hypervigilance.
  I must prepare to leave with diligence.

9/18/2020

We had thirty-one straight days of Spare the Air days, with air quality ranging up to very unhealthy or even hazardous on some days. I check the air quality index (AQI) before walking. Fires continue to rage out of control in some areas, more than five weeks after the dry lightning storms that sparked large blazes up and down our state. We are also getting smoke from fires in tinder-dry Oregon and Washington. Our blue skies will not last long! All national parks in our state except Yosemite were closed yesterday.

The Diablo Winds that plague us in late summer or autumn sometimes gust up to 90 mph in higher elevations. Those winds during bone-dry conditions greatly heighten fire danger and the need for quick evacuation. PG&E sometimes turns off power for several days so that damaged power lines don't spark a wildfire, as in the tragedy of Paradise, California.

CALIFORNIA, THEN AND NOW

The cerulean skies today cheer me,
Like the heavenly skies I used to see –
Absent of haze or dense smoke in the air.
If only it could be so everywhere.
My adopted state changed since we arrived.
Bob and I moved here after '65.
Forests were healthy and camping was great.
In California, much to celebrate!
San Francisco had no homeless camped out.
Traffic was minimal, without a doubt.
Good jobs and housing were plentiful then.
Too many people from elsewhere moved in.
  The California dream has come apart,
  But I still love it here with all my heart.

9/22/2020

The population more than doubled in California since 1966 when we moved here from France, after working for the U.S. military.

Droughts, leading to forest fires and wildfires destroying entire communities, have become commonplace. I recently installed air-conditioning in my house. Any time of year our days can be unseasonably warm. Fog is less frequent and dense here. PG&E public service power shutoffs happen regularly when fire danger is high or when energy production is inadequate.

Homelessness and squalor are often seen in California's major cities. Los Angeles, Oakland, and San Francisco are among the worst. During this COVID emergency, many homeless have been moved into shelters or temporary housing. COVID-19 is making our state's problems much worse.

RIP RUTH BADER GINSBURG

"The Notorious RBG" is dead.
Our nation is in a state of mourning.
This sad event fills progressives with dread,
'Tho her cancer's return gave us warning.
Ginsburg was a champion of women's rights
To reproductive choice and equal pay.
This feisty woman led principled fights
That she argued with skill to win the day.
The shameless Republicans could not wait
For two hours after she took her last breath
To announce what she feared would be her fate,
They would soon fill the seat left by her death.
    Our nation has reached a crossroads today.
    We must fight to preserve our USA!

9/20/2020

Ruth Bader Ginsburg, 87, was appointed by President Bill Clinton. She served faithfully on the U.S. Supreme Court from 1993 until her death yesterday from pancreatic cancer. She fought valiantly to survive until the election was over, but pancreatic cancer is a formidable foe – the worst she had ever encountered in her tenure as a Supreme Court Justice. Although she fought cancer several times and suffered various orthopedic problems, Ginsburg never missed any time in Court before the age of 85. She knew how to disagree with dignity and class without alienating those on the opposite side.

Chief Justice John Roberts said of Ginsburg: "Our nation has lost a cherished colleague. Today we mourn, but with confidence that future generations will remember Ruth Bader Ginsburg as we knew her – a tireless and resolute champion of justice."

UNPRESIDENTIAL DEBATE

The debate tonight proved a debacle,
With Trump bullying and interrupting.
He turned it into a sorry spectacle,
Determined to continue disrupting.
Joe Biden arrived completely prepared
To explain his well-thought-out positions.
Trump blustered and appeared as though impaired
As he carried out his inquisitions.
The personal attacks began to fly,
Which the moderator couldn't prevent.
Throughout it all, Trump continued to lie,
Flouting procedures given their consent.
    This "debate" was a national disgrace.
    It's obvious who we need to replace!

9/29/2020

Moderator Chris Wallace of Fox News could not handle the obstreperous president.

Memorable lines from the debate:
Biden: "It is what it is, because you are who you are." (speaking of the pandemic)

Trump: "Stand back and stand by." Speaking to the Proud Boys and/or other white supremacist groups. They already had signs and T-shirts under production!

CORONAVIRUS KARMA

His karma caught up with Trump at warp speed
For outrages he has perpetrated.
Marine One has flown him to Walter Reed,
In case he would need to be intubated.
Last night the results of his COVID test
Appeared as a shock on the nightly news.
He will stay "a few days" where care is best,
After propagating untruthful views.
En route, he appeared in a suit and *mask*,
Which he'd often mocked others for wearing.
Reassuring his voters was his task,
As our nation *guessed* how he was faring.
  Trump *must* be ill if he isn't tweeting.
  At fault, no masks and closely-packed seating.

10/2/2020

Trump often declared COVID-19 a "hoax" perpetrated by Democrats. He withheld the extent and lethality of COVID-19 from the public. This week, he claimed falsely that we had "turned the corner" on COVID. U.S. cases are rising alarmingly, with over 209,000 persons dying since its inception and over 7 million infected. He has advocated opening up the country and letting "herd immunity" guide policy. Trump has muzzled his scientific experts and perhaps caused statistics to be misrepresented.

News of Trump's "positive" COVID test came after learning that White House Aide Hope Hicks had tested positive for the disease after traveling and attending meetings with him. At least ten persons closely associated with Trump, including Kelly Ann Conway and Chris Christie, now have COVID. Close contact and no masks during debate prep and the Rose Garden celebration of Amy Coney Barrett's Supreme Court nomination are suspected of causing contagion among staff, supporters, and Senators.

PHYSICIAN SPIN

Americans need to be told the truth
Regarding our President's condition.
Such deceptions I recall from my youth
When we were misled by a physician.
His doctor, an osteopath, said today
He wanted to give a positive spin,
Admitting some data was wrong to convey,
And then he walked some of it back again.
Trump's case of COVID was worse than we knew
As reported by his own chief of staff.
ER doctors on TV gave us a clue
That what Dr. Conley told us was chaff.
    People must know now as voting takes place
    Which leader would be the best to embrace.

10/4/2020

Apparently, Dr. Sean Conley, Trump's personal physician, is aware that his patient is monitoring the TV coverage on his condition. Medical reports have been directed to "an audience of one" so as not to enrage Trump and "cause him to have a downturn."

Trump pulled an outrageous caper today. Although quite ill and still contagious, he got his way and entered a van to be driven by two Secret Service persons wearing full PPE so that he could wave to his supporters. He is frustrated at being unable to campaign during the final four weeks before the election. Early voting is already taking place in some states.

Trump is on three powerful drugs: monoclonal antibodies still in clinical trials, Remdesivir and Dexamethasone, a steroid that can cause MANIA! He refuses to turn over the reins to Pence!

INCORRIGIBLE

Trump is a six-foot-three petulant child.
It's pointless to attempt to control him.
While growing up, he was known to be wild,
His demeanor determined on a whim.
Now in his seventies, little has changed.
He won't observe traditions or the rules.
Shunning COVID protocols, he acts deranged.
He considers those complying as fools.
He refused to stay confined at Walter Reed,
Taking a "joy ride" to wave to his fans.
His purpose, looking strong on the news feed!
All his doctors deferred to his demands.
We know so little about this disease.
Did doctors release him early to please?

10/7/2020

After reading *Too Much and Never Enough* by Trump's clinical psychologist niece Mary L. Trump, PhD, I understood more about the emotional deficits of Donald's formative years. She believes that his early deprivation of love and understanding produced the warped person who, for a time, became the most powerful leader in the world.

There was speculation about whether Trump might still be contagious after his discharge from Walter Reed National Military Medical Center. He received only three days of treatment before returning to the White House. Some attributed his early release to "VIP syndrome."

UNHINGED

If Trump's state of mind seems to be manic,
Is that good reason for us to panic?
His COVID illness and strong medications
May worsen his brain; we see indications.
Where is Mike Pence when he needs to stand by?
Holding large rallies with more who will die!
Time to talk of the 25th Amendment;
Pressure is building in public sentiment.
Trump's behavior and tweets are more erratic.
Our country needs change, we are emphatic!
Joe Biden continues to increase his lead.
He is the kind of leader we need.
  Trump's steroid treatments place us in danger.
  Each day, his ravings have become stranger.

10/6/2020

Trump is on three strong drugs: experimental Monoclonal Antibodies, Remdesivir, and Dexamethasone (a steroid that can cause mania, delusions of grandeur, and otherwise distort the thinking process). These drugs have probably never been used in combination before on anyone else.

VICE PRESIDENTIAL CANDIDATES FACE OFF

This debate setup had never been seen,
With Harris and Pence spaced twelve feet apart
And Plexiglas sheets between them to screen
From COVID droplets that speech could impart.
Ms. Page *tried* hard to keep Pence's words timed,
Held to minutes allotted, on topic.
Kamala's sharp jabs were often inclined
To critique COVID handling as *myopic.*
The audience was warned of ejection
For those who didn't adhere to the rules.
No applause throughout or face mask rejection
And newly tested for COVID – good tools.
  At the conclusion, as candidates bickered,
  A fly landed on Pence as people snickered.

10/8/2020

Susan Page was the moderator. She tried hard and sometimes succeeded in holding Pence to the topic and time limits.

The fly that perched on and almost got stuck on Pence's lacquered hair provided some moments of levity and reflection about its significance:

"Recognizing BS responses when it saw it."

UNREPENTANT SURVIVOR

His brush with death left Donald Trump unchanged.
With COVID-19, he got the best care.
The steroids given made him more deranged,
With drug combos never used anywhere.
Trump was flown by chopper to Walter Reed
With fever and difficulty breathing.
The staff ministered to his every need,
But his doctor's reports were misleading.
Within ten days, he was back campaigning,
"I might now be immune," he told his fans.
"Don't let COVID control you!" and complaining,
"Masks are harmful. Not needed in the stands."
　New COVID clusters will shortly follow.
　Fans will see that his advice was hollow.

10/18/2020

Trump may still have been contagious when he first embarked on his campaign touring. Was he contagious during the debate with Joe Biden? No one will reveal his last "negative" test.

All of Trump's rallies are packing people in, shoulder to shoulder, and most not wearing masks. Shouting and cheering in the stands – a prescription for disaster. Cases continue to rise alarmingly across the country. The third COVID-19 wave is rolling in and may soon swamp our healthcare facilities. We have hit 8 million cases!

Why has it become almost a badge of honor and a symbol of personal freedom among Trump supporters not to wear masks? Our *Dear Leader* sets the tone! One would think he would have changed after he, wife Melania and son Barron got COVID.

SLEEPLESS IN OAKLAND

I feel in shock, and my head is swimming.
My ballot is cast, with two weeks to go.
Can I trust the polls with Biden winning?
Each day, the Trump rallies reach a new low.
Like a rabid dog, Trump's in attack mode.
He targets Fauci for telling the truth
While stoking white "Proud Boys," speaking in code;
Spreading wild conspiracies with no proof.
Two blue state governors fear for their lives
With Trump inflaming passions against them.
Silently lurking, COVID spreads and thrives.
Prospects for quick containment appear dim.
    I pray this national nightmare will end.
    Joe Biden could help our country to mend.

10/20/2020

The governors of Oregon and Michigan had violent passions stirred up against them by Trump.

I voted by absentee ballot and deposited it in a secure drop box.
I got an email confirming my ballot had been received and counted.
I was ecstatic! It was much safer to vote absentee during COVID-19.

Trump is trying to convince his base that voting by mail is a fraud. The bulk of his voters will go to the polls on Election Day. Therefore, early polls will probably indicate that Trump won, as it takes extra time to tally and report all the voting by mail and military ballots from overseas posts. This administration has tried to disenfranchise voters by removing postal boxes from minority neighborhoods and by dismantling many postal sorting machines.

OBAMA'S TAKEDOWN OF TRUMP

Obama's critique of Trump was scathing,
Launching salvoes he must have been saving
For such a moment on the campaign trail.
The Biden Train can't be left to derail!
He blamed Trump for the COVID emergency –
For freezing, not acting with urgency.
Ignoring guidelines that are widely known,
"He couldn't protect himself or his own."
Hurling choice barbs, he labeled Trump lazy.
His insults surely drove Donald crazy.
"Trump only looks out for himself and friends.
We must vote to see that his regime ends."
  Obama's oratory was on display;
  His skills in prosecution carried the day.

10/22/2020

Barack Obama was our 44th President of the United States. He was charismatic, respected internationally, and the first African-American president of our country. A Democrat, he met with considerable obstruction in the Senate from Republican Majority Leader Mitch McConnell of Kentucky. McConnell would frequently decline to bring important legislation to the floor for a vote. In frustration, Obama began issuing Executive Orders. Donald Trump would later emulate that practice, in which he did considerable harm to our nation and environment. Fortunately, those orders are reversable by the next president. Obama's signature legislation was the Affordable Care Act, under which many more Americans were able to access medical care.

Obama was usually restrained in criticizing other leaders in the past, but in campaigning for his former, beloved Vice President Joe Biden, he pulled out all the stops and let loose on Trump.

DONNY COVIDSEED

Rallies are seeding the virus widely
Featuring Donny at numerous sites.
Adoring crowds are packed in unwisely.
Who can explain the throngs Trump delights?
He exposes fans to rain, heat or cold,
Without concern for how they are faring.
Many will fall ill because they are old.
He continues to downplay mask wearing.
At his rallies, some needed a medic,
Transported for hospitalization.
His disregard for others is pathetic.
Yet, people attend with no hesitation.
   The seeds of disease that Donny has spread
   Will show up soon as countless more dead.

10/30/2020

Donny Covidseed is President Donald Trump!

While the legend of Johnny "Appleseed" suggests that his planting was random, there was actually a firm economic basis for John Chapman's behavior. He established nurseries and returned, after several years, to sell off the orchard and the surrounding land. The trees that Johnny Chapman planted had multiple purposes, although they did not yield edible fruit. The small, tart apples his orchards produced were useful primarily to make hard cider and applejack. Orchards also served the critical legal purpose of establishing land claims along the frontier. As a consequence, Chapman owned around 1,200 acres of valuable land at the time of his death.

ELECTION DAY

This day we dreamed of has at last arrived
When we might restore what earlier thrived,
Our exceptional land of liberty,
A shining beacon of diversity.
My heart beats faster today with great pride.
The voice of our people cannot be denied.
We've learned to treasure our proud legacy.
Let's again light our lamp for the world to see.
After stress and worries of the past four years,
Let us put away strong hatreds and fears.
We have learned hard lessons we mustn't forget.
The world will see our future is bright yet!
    Today, our Lady Liberty has smiled.
    The vast majority can't be beguiled!

11/3/2020

I feel optimistic about what this day may bring. I pray that my intuition is right!

I should re-name my poem Election *Week*, as votes are still being counted three days later, and it might not conclude until next week. By November 6, we could see that Joe Biden is headed for the Presidency. If all goes as predicted, I will be ecstatic! There is so much at stake!

JOYFUL DAY!

To what can I compare this joyful day?
My graduation from North Texas State;
My flight to Turkey for a one-year stay;
Falling in love there with my future mate.
Our Berlin engagement in the fallen snow;
Changing assignments from Berlin to France;
Touring Europe, before De Gaulle said "Go;"
Finding new work in Oakland in advance.
Exploring our fair city and new state;
Taking our newborns to our Montclair home;
Pollock Pines for holidays to celebrate;
Our hikes in forests where we loved to roam.
The day that Victor came to live with me;
Rejoicing at Barack Obama's win;
I wish that Victor had been here to see
The defeat of Trump by Joseph Biden.
    On this day we saved our democracy
    From the clutches of Trump's autocracy.

11/7/2020

Five days after the November 3rd election, Joe Biden was finally declared President-Elect! Due to COVID-19, many ballots will be counted for a few weeks. An avalanche of absentee voting came in, mostly by Democrats and Independents. Those large-volume votes and overseas ballots had to be carefully counted. Teams of Democrats, Republicans and Independents were tabulating and overseeing the process. Nevertheless, Trump cried "fraud" and "stolen election," as anticipated. He mounted over sixty ridiculous lawsuits and threatened to take his case to the Supreme Court. He declared himself the winner on Election Day and refused to concede when the race was called for Biden. Today, I think of celebrations when the Berlin Wall came down in 1989.

THE POLITICS OF PRESIDENTIAL PETULANCE

"He who rides a tiger fears to dismount."
That Chinese proverb rings so true today.
Spineless men support Trump's futile recount,
But outsized margins for Biden will stay.
In or out of office, Trump's a danger.
Will he sell our country's information?
Every day our politics grow stranger,
While COVID advances decimation.
Most aggravating, Trump has not conceded.
He tweets and pouts and glowers silently.
His staff will not admit he's been defeated.
We pray this standoff won't end violently.
  This week, key military staffing changed.
  Each day Trump seems more totally deranged.

(My title is a phrase I heard Brian Williams use last night on MSNBC.)

11/12/2020

Ch'i 'hu nan hsia pei goes the Chinese proverb, translated in 1875 as, "He who rides a tiger is afraid to **dismount**." The Oxford Dictionary of Proverbs interprets the old Asian metaphor as, "Once a dangerous or troublesome venture is begun, the safest course is to carry it through to the end."

Many of the world's leaders have called Joe Biden to congratulate him on his victory, but Secretary of State Pompeo, Attorney General Bill Barr, and other key staff continue to perpetuate the fiction that Trump won. Especially troubling, capable Secretary of Defense Mark Esper was fired this week and replaced with a Trump sycophant.

REVIVING SPIRITS

Tonight I sit before my cheerful fire.
A sense of calm is settling over me.
I feel relief at what I've seen transpire
Since news of Joseph Biden's victory.
I think of people dancing in the street
With joyfulness that they could not contain.
Although protests occur on Trump's defeat,
The ballot recounts will proceed in vain.
The state of denial soon will tumble down
Brick by brick like the fallen Berlin Wall.
Once the electors vote as they are bound,
Biden will be the leader for us all.
  Despite the fears I've harbored this tense week,
  My spirits rise when Biden and Klain speak.

11/12/2020

Update: Today, November 12, Arizona declared Joe Biden to be the winner for President. (The state of Georgia also would name Biden the winner the following day.)

Ron Klain was selected as Joe Biden's Chief of Staff. He was the perfect pick. He served as chief of staff for two previous vice-presidents. Klain successfully led efforts to contain the Ebola pandemic, and he was instrumental in assisting the revival of the economy under our 44th President Barack Obama. Taking office in January 2009, Obama inherited a terrible economy (The Great Recession) that required major efforts to successfully turn around.

Donald Trump has still not conceded!

NIGHTMARE SCENARIO FOR JOE BIDEN

Now we know why Trump dismissed Mark Esper.
He's pulling half our troops from Afghanistan.
Esper warned of terror plots to deter.
Trump might order missile strikes on Iran.
With barely two months left in his regime,
Trump's wielding a wrecking ball while he may.
Each day we struggle through a frightful dream
As pillars of democracy decay.
Ms. Murphy won't sign off on the transition.
The clearances Joe needs cannot proceed.
COVID teams *must* meet without restriction.
Can no authority now intercede?
　Meanwhile, Trump is demanding recounting
　While the pressures on Biden are mounting.

11/19/2020

Trump fired Secretary of Defense Mark Esper days after he lost the election. He refuses to let the normal transition take place and is obstructing Biden from planning with his incoming team. Trump won't concede, insisting to followers that he will remain in office.

On November 14, there was a massive "Stop the Steal" rally in D.C. with throngs of unmasked Trump supporters who choose to believe lies that the Democrats stole the election. Joe Biden now has 306 electoral votes, considered "a landslide" when Trump achieved that number in 2016. Biden won Georgia and Arizona recently.

After weeks of resistance, GSA Administrator Emily Murphy on 11/24 gave consent to President-elect Joe Biden to begin his transition to the White House. He now has access to Presidential Briefings and the COVID-19 Task Force.

MY CHRISTMAS WISHES

"Joy to the World" may ring hollow this year.
I'm *trying* to display my Christmas cheer.
May we soon see an end to our isolation
And once more have cause for true celebration.
"Joy to the World" this Christmas means to me
The gift of new vaccines which promise victory
Over COVID-19, that stealthy foe
That has caused the world unspeakable woe.
May the New Year bring us a much better year
When we can return to living without fear.
May health and good fortune arrive at your door,
Bringing safety to gather with loved ones once more.

11/21/2020

My 2020 Christmas Letter
What I Did in the Time of COVID-19

Staying home alone
Talking on the phone
Hearing somber news
On Facebook sharing views
Walking up my street
Preparing food to eat
Shopping with Instacart
Writing from my heart
Zooming with family and friends
Waiting 'till this ends
Music, films and reading
Expert advice, I'm heeding!

SUPREME COURT REBUKE

Hooray! Hooray! Justice was served today.
Nine High Court justices turned Trump's case down.
He wanted key votes to be thrown away.
Lawyer Giuliani was a strange clown.
Trump is still rejecting Joe Biden's win.
His party refuses to say "He lost."
He threatens in four years to run again.
Turmoil he stirs up will come at great cost!
Meanwhile, he's raising hard cash from his fans
And raving to all about how he won.
He holds unmasked rallies in the packed stands.
In forty-two days, his tenure is done!
    Today Trump earned great humiliation
    Based on no legal justification.

12/8/2020

This rebuke must have been especially humiliating to Trump since three of the newest judges were put on the Supreme Court through his own nominating process.

In another strange but predictable twist, Trump's lead attorney, Rudy Giuliani, in pressing his many lawsuits, is now hospitalized with COVID-19. He has rarely been seen wearing a mask.

Today was also "Safe Harbor Day," after which the Electoral College votes for each state cannot be overturned. On Monday, the official Electoral College vote counts will be taken. Afterward, there can be no further contesting of this election in which Biden earned 306 Electoral College votes and over seven million in the popular vote.

MAKE A JOYFUL NOISE!

Today is such a significant day
As COVID may soon start to melt away.
The first vaccines are now being received,
Although some worry they're being deceived.
Also important, the electors meet.
Their voting should seal a complete defeat
For Trump and his minions drawing things out
While Donald continues to fume and pout.
How sad, many Trumpists believe *he* won.
When will they see this election is done?
Joe Biden has won this race fair and square.
There is so much he must try to repair!
  I awoke once more with hope in my heart.
  Our nation and world can see a new start.

12/14/2020

The poem's title is taken from Psalm 100:

"Make a joyful noise to the Lord, all ye lands!
Serve the Lord with gladness!
Come into his presence with singing!....

Enter his gates with thanksgiving,
And his courts with praise!
Give thanks to him, bless his name!..."

OUTRAGE

Donald Trump is guilty of *sedition*,
Now trying to undo an election
With use of force to keep his position,
Unless there is serious defection.
He declares the election was stolen
Which many followers now still believe.
Some Republicans may feel beholden.
The tragic outcome is hard to conceive.
Now pardoned, Mike Flynn suggests using troops.
Radical groups are poised to cause conflict.
The next month will reveal how low Trump stoops.
What harms to our country will he inflict?
  This crisis we are watching now unfold
  Are actions by Trump that many foretold.

12/22/2020

Sedition is overt conduct, such as speech and organization, that tends toward rebellion against the established order. Sedition often includes subversion of a constitution and incitement of discontent toward, or rebellion against, established authority. Sedition may include any commotion, though not aimed at direct and open violence against the laws. Seditious words in writing are seditious libel. A seditionist is one who engages in or promotes the interest of sedition.

Former General Mike Flynn, whom Trump recently pardoned, called for **martial law** to enforce new elections in key swing states while taking control of ballots already cast.

CHRISTMAS CHAOS

This Christmas Eve, things are up in the air
As the world is plunged into deep despair.
Millions travel, though COVID is surging
Heedless of cautions health experts are urging.
Our government stands in full disarray.
All funding is hung up, to our dismay.
No stimulus checks for those in distress
Or vaccine funding, enough to depress.
Trump has departed for Mar-a-Lago
Where he blusters and threatens to veto
The package that Congress has enacted.
Unexpected, the way he reacted.
    Trump's callous behavior holds no precedent.
    Hasten the day he's no longer president!

12/24/2020

HAZARDOUS TRAVEL

Why are so many people traveling
During this Christmas holiday season
While society is unraveling?
I couldn't think of a valid reason.
Newly diagnosed COVID is surging.
Doctors are turning some patients away.
Why don't folks follow the experts' urging?
Loved ones could live to see a better day.
We must decide we're in this together.
Your thoughtless actions could affect me, too.
Take your vaccine to protect you better,
Then follow the guidelines given to you.
  After we put this virus in its place
  We can all once more be free to embrace.

12/31/2020

Now there is a new, more contagious strain of COVID-19 found present in Colorado and California, originally detected in England. The Pfizer vaccine rollout has begun, but on this last day of 2020, only about 3 million of the 20 million Pfizer doses promised by year's end have been administered, mostly to healthcare workers and first responders. Next will be elderly persons in nursing homes.

Los Angeles hospitals are in crisis, filled beyond capacity, with one person dying about every 10 seconds. Still, ambulances arrive with new critically ill persons. Doctors must initiate a painful triage to decide who has the best chance of survival and who they can't help.

Trump says that the federal government got vaccines developed and delivered to the states. Now, it's *up to the states* to administer the vaccines. Biden will soon implement a federal, coordinated effort.

HOPE

As I sit before my gas log fireplace,
I bask in its warmth and watch light rain fall.
Tomorrow will conclude the Senate race
When our nation's fate will be clear to all.
I'm hopeful that the Democrats can win
With Ossoff and Warnock in the tight race.
We'd gain control of the Senate again.
McConnell's tenure has been a disgrace.
Trump's urgent, taped phone call just came to light.
He tried to change the Georgia election.
Our president is frightened of his plight.
His threats were met by a firm rejection.
    In just sixteen days Donald Trump will leave.
    Biden will be a leader we can believe.

1/4/2021

In a taped phone call on January 2 made by President Trump to Georgia Secretary of State Brad Raffensperger, he tried for an hour to exert pressure to **"find 11,780 votes"** to make himself the winner of the Georgia election. That total would be *one more vote* than Biden had. Trump is joined on the call by White House Chief of Staff Mark Meadows. The Georgia Republican, who *voted for Trump,* said he could do no such thing. He stood his ground admirably. In his anticipation of this kind of illegal request, Raffensperger had the entire call recorded.

JUBILATION

This morning I'm feeling jubilation!
Biden can work to restore our nation.
On Tuesday the voters of Georgia spoke.
Mitch McConnell's iron rule we can revoke!
With Warnock and Ossoff, the balance shifted.
Our new senators-elect are gifted.
Stacy Abrams helped to turn out the vote.
Her work has been praised by Democrats of note.
Today we see democracy in action.
Our nation rejected an evil faction.
Some may try to stir up insurrection.
We continue working toward perfection.
    Let Trump slink away in abject disgrace.
    It's such a relief not to see his face.

1/6/2021

The Rev. Raphael Warnock is pastor of Ebenezer Baptist Church, where Martin Luther King Jr. was once the pastor. He will be Georgia's first Black Senator and the first from the South. Jon Ossoff, the son of Jewish immigrants, will be the youngest U.S. Senator at thirty-three.

Mitch McConnell, current Speaker of the U.S. House, won't bring progressive legislation to the floor. He recently opposed the $2,000 in stimulus checks to help families struggling through COVID-19, even though Trump supported it at the last minute.

Today, counting and certification of Electoral College votes takes place in the Senate, normally a perfunctory process. Numerous Republicans are mounting efforts to overturn minorities' votes in battleground states and to substitute other electors. Trump expects Vice President Pence to manage the process so that *he* is declared winner instead of Joe Biden. This effort is doomed to failure, but it harms democracy.

INCITEMENT

Trump has incited full insurrection
While Congress convened to confirm the election.
Unruly mobs breached the Capitol grounds.
Their brash and brazen encroachment astounds!
Trump encouraged their disgraceful actions.
He stoked the flames in these radical factions.
The workings of government came to a halt.
He has refused to acknowledge his fault.
At last, he told the protestors, "Go Home."
But continued to lie in tweets from his phone.
"The election was stolen," he again claimed.
Our nation's reputation has been defamed!
  Trump is a danger that must be contained.
  He should be removed from time that remains.

1/6/2021

Vandals broke into the Capitol Building on this critical day when election results were being certified. Senators and Representatives had to be secretly evacuated. "Protestors" swarmed into the halls and rooms of our revered "citadel of liberty" where dedicated public servants were doing the people's business. This is the first time the U.S. Capitol has been breached since the War of 1812 by the British.

Police protection and Capitol Police were totally inadequate. The National Guard from several states was eventually called in to try to control the situation. At least one woman was critically shot in the chest during the mob's storming and swarming. Five persons were killed on that shameful day! A curfew for 6 pm was issued.

Rioters had put up a noose and were shouting, "Hang Mike Pence!" due to Trump's strong criticism of him. The president never tried to stop the invasion, in which his own vice president was at great risk.

COMMENDATIONS FOR CONGRESS

On Tuesday, Congress was magnificent.
Trump-inspired mob actions made some repent.
Despite the chilling assault on the Capitol
They returned to work in their cherished hall.
The shocking invasion caused defections.
Some Republicans dropped their objections,
Letting vote certification proceed.
They proclaimed Joe Biden elected, indeed!
Trump's infamous coup attempt had backfired.
His critics are current staff and retired.
Yesterday, our Congress came together,
Counting down days that they must still weather.
    A few Republicans advocate action.
    Plans to remove Trump are gaining traction.

1/7/2021

Facebook and Twitter are beginning to limit Trump's access! There is talk of suspending his Twitter account indefinitely.

Under consideration is a second impeachment or use of the 25th Amendment in which the Vice President would initiate Trump's removal from office.

MORTIFICATION

This week our nation has been horrified
By the Capitol building incursion.
Around the globe we have been mortified
By our president's act of subversion.
Our country's reputation has been harmed
By this breach of our seat of democracy –
With numerous vandals inside, some armed,
Riled up in support of autocracy.
Our foes gloat at our humiliation
While our friends look upon us with pity.
This attack was an act of desecration
By those called to our nation's fair city.
  Our president now has blood on his hands
  For inciting rough and unruly bands.

1/8/2021

Trump had called upon his Twitter followers to convene in D.C. on January 6 to support him and to protest against the "stolen election." He tweeted in advance, "Be there. It will be WILD!"

Growing numbers of brazen intruders are being identified from photos, videos and social media posts. Ringleaders appear to be Proud Boys, white supremacists, QAnon conspiracy advocates, anti-Semites, and other dangerous terrorist and white nationalist groups. Because they were so outnumbered, Capitol Police ushered most persons out without making arrests.

Five persons died in the riotous insurrection, including one Capitol policeman assaulted with a fire extinguisher and bear spray, and a QAnon advocate, shot as she tried to break through doors to the chambers. Areas inside were trashed and souvenirs were taken. Documents confirming Electoral College votes had been evacuated.

HIGH ANXIETY

When did I last feel so anxious and fearful
For our nation's fate that made me tearful?
The day the New York Twin Towers came down.
I watched as the second tower hit the ground.
The Cuban Missile Crisis left me stunned.
After thirteen tense days, the day was won.
Soon after, JFK was shot in Texas,
I cried and prayed to God to protect us!
A few years later, we lost MLK,
Closely followed by the death of RFK.
That terrible day I stayed in my bed
When I should have taught my classes instead.
    This week was also a heart-felt trauma,
    When marauders sparked the Capitol drama.

1/8/2021

I shudder to think how devastating and destructive this event *could have been* on Wednesday, January 6. House and Senate members and Vice President Pence were in the Capitol tallying Electoral College votes to declare official results of the November election. All had to be evacuated after countless rioters broke into the sacred U.S. Capitol space and wreaked havoc throughout. Six hours later, members of Congress and Vice President Pence returned to finish their business – at 4 a.m.

President Trump fired up the crowd at a morning rally, telling them to descend upon the Capitol. He exhorted them to be strong and to boldly make their grievances known. Many Trump followers believed his frequent lies that the election was stolen. He told them he would be staying in office, if only they would fight for him. Others knew the truth but welcomed the chance to create chaos! About 8,000 of them descended upon the poorly guarded "Citadel of our Democracy."

MISCREANTS

Our society is troubled today
By numerous deluded deviants
With their ill will this week on full display –
A collection of thuggish miscreants.
They turned their wrath on our nation's Congress,
Gathered in the Capitol we revere,
The peaceful transfer of power to address.
They must see punishments that are severe!
Our eyes were opened to see the riffraff
As the rampaged through the Capitol's halls.
Their mission, to disrupt and to harm key staff.
Ejected *this time*, they issued new calls!
  Trump has incited this revolution.
  We must come up with an urgent solution!

1/9/2021

House Speaker Nancy Pelosi issued these options regarding Trump: 1) His resignation; 2) Removal from office under the 25th Amendment; 3) A second impeachment initiated in the House. Impeachment and conviction would bar him from holding a federal office again. Mitch McConnell refuses to schedule an impeachment hearing in the Senate until January 19th, *the day before Trump would be out of office.*

This Capitol incursion was even more threatening than it first appeared. Some intruders were chanting "Hang Mike Pence!" because he refused to substitute electors' votes that would give Trump a second term. A noose and platform were found, along with zip ties for handcuffs, bombs, and some "MAGA Mafia" were armed. They took correspondence and laptops, but failed to find Electoral College votes. Invaders located offices of House Whip James Clyburn and Speaker Nancy Pelosi, perhaps using *inside sources* to find their way through the labyrinth.

HEARTACHE AT THE CAPITOL

My heart aches for the country I love
And brave defenders who withstood the mob.
Our nation's leaders were protected from above.
Despite great duress, Mike Pence did his job.
They hid under desks and donned a gas mask
Before being led to a safer place,
Vowing to come back to complete their task.
Not all wore a face mask in the tight space.
What courage they showed to return to their hall
To resume vote counts and confirm Biden's win
After the building was secured by nightfall,
While horrors they went through still haunted within.
    Today they honored the officer who died.
    His family can view his actions with pride.

1/10/2021

"**Officer Sicknick** is an American hero who gave his life defending our Capitol, and our nation will never forget or fail to honor the service and sacrifice of Officer Brian Sicknick." – V.P. Mike Pence

Officer Brian Sicknick, 42, died of his injuries after being assaulted using a fire extinguisher and bear spray during the mob's rampages. The White House refused to lower the flag to half-mast until the day of the funeral.

Health authorities are predicting this Capitol attack will prove to have been a super-spreader event. Two Republicans refused offers of a mask while sequestered closely together in a confined space. It is almost miraculous that Senate and House members and staff escaped serious harm. All were urged to get a COVID-19 test after their sequestration together.

LIFE SUPPORT

The inauguration is under threat.
I'm wondering how much worse things can get.
Trump's staunch supporters have infiltrated
Key groups that want Democrats subjugated.
Police, armed forces and legislatures
May be infected with perpetrators
Who stop at nothing to accomplish ends
That harm democracy and alarm our friends.
My elation at Biden's election
Is dampened due to diehards' rejection
Of the rightful president of our land.
Their obstructions can't be allowed to stand.
    Our democracy is on life support
    Due to homegrown terrorists we can't deport!

1/12/2021

Retired General Barry McCaffrey stated on MSNBC last night that he has grave reservations about holding the Inauguration of Joe Biden in an open-air setting. He believes it will be difficult to provide the security needed. Perhaps we need a virtual inauguration this year. State capitals across the country have also been warned of possible armed incursions in all 50 states, beginning on January 16.

About a dozen Capitol Police have been suspended and are being investigated for their roles, including cooperation and possible collusion with domestic terrorists, in the January 6th invasion of the Capitol. One wore a MAGA hat (Make America Great Again). Others posed for selfies.

Three Democratic Senators are now testing positive for COVID-19, after having to sequester with several Republicans who refused to wear a mask during the dire emergency. More cases could follow.

COMIC RELIEF

While I'm viewing news from the FBI
I enjoy the squirrels that sprint and cavort.
On a day like this one I'd like to cry,
But images of nature warm my heart.
When overcast clears with sun's warming rays,
Resident squirrels love to play on my lawn.
I try to relax as I count the days
Until Donald Trump will shortly be gone!
My furry friends are consoling today.
They dig in my yard to find buried treats.
Can they see my amusement as they play?
Their agile movements are amazing feats.
    The creatures I'm watching haven't a clue
    Of the worries affecting me and you.

1/12/2021

Observing my squirrels and backyard birds, as well as spending time in my garden, make life more enjoyable during these days of isolation and sheltering at home from COVID-19. These activities also allow me to better cope with the barrage of bad news coming out each day.

RAYS OF SUNLIGHT

Strong rays of sun have broken through the gloom.
Now Mitch McConnell is singing in tune.
He and Nancy have agreed to impeach.
I feared that action would be out of reach.
It seems *some* Republicans want this purging
After hearing Democrats' strong urging.
"Impeach and Remove" would ban Trump from serving
And cut off his perks as undeserving.
Videos showing unruly mob action
Caused key Republications to voice retraction.
The evidence is there for all to see.
Trump and radicals betrayed our country.
  The world may soon breathe a sigh of relief.
  How we traveled this road is beyond belief!

1/12/2021

Speaker of the House Nancy Pelosi is a savvy and persuasive politician. In addition, violent videos showing desecration of the Capitol and the attacks on law enforcement and our nation's leaders have repeatedly aired on the news since the despicable incursion on January 6. Public opinion was beginning to turn against Republicans.

When key Republicans such as Liz Cheney spoke out for Trump's removal, Senate Majority Leader Mitch McConnell listened. I'm not a supporter of McConnell, but he can be astute. His wife Elaine Chao resigned as Transportation Secretary soon after the attack took place.

STAINED LEGACY: TWICE IMPEACHED

"It's not a stain, it's now a tattoo."
The Congress now knows what they must do.
The House and Senate proceed to impeach
Especially after Trump's recent speech.
In Alamo, Texas visiting the Wall
Trump once more refused to answer the call
To repent of his words to incite a mob
In order to try to stay in his job.
The House is opening hearings today.
Both parties may unite to put Trump away.
He must be held to account for his actions
In his alliance with violent factions.
　It's poignant to see this meeting take place.
　Donald Trump's regime has been a disgrace.

1/13/2021

I heard this comment on MSNBC this morning from Chuck Todd. It is a perfect opening line for my poem.

On this day, it is precisely one week since the violent and bloody invasion of the Capitol Building in Washington, D.C. on the day the Electoral College votes were to be counted and certified. All week, we have seen videos of the brutality and desecration that took place on that day. People who recognize participants in the insurrection at the Capitol are calling the FBI to identify them.

Third-ranking Republican in the House, Liz Cheney, came out in support of impeachment yesterday stating, "This was the biggest betrayal of our Constitution and country by any U.S. President in our history."

THE BRIGHT SIDE

Many encouraging things have occurred,
Despite the violent attack in D.C.
That same day, on the 6th, we got the word
We'd won the prized Senate majority.
When both Perdue and Loeffler conceded,
Rejoicing for Georgia was hard to contain.
Ossoff and Warnock couldn't be defeated.
Stacey Abrams' efforts were not in vain.
In more than sixty court cases appealed,
The judges displayed their integrity.
The Supreme Court verdict also revealed
That Trump could not win with Giuliani.
   Trump failed to overturn the election.
   His orders to Pence were met with rejection.

1/14/2021

Rudy Giuliani spearheaded legal efforts for Donald Trump by appealing vote tallies to battleground state courts and to the Supreme Court. He lost every single case. He did not testify under oath about election fraud, as he knew that doing so would expose himself to perjury charges.

Stacey Abrams has worked tirelessly in Georgia to register and engage Black voters in the political process. She was narrowly defeated for governor a few years ago. Since then, her single-minded focus has been to change politics in Georgia through demonstrating to Black communities their power at the polls to influence positive change in their lives. Georgia was flipped from Red to a Blue with the 2020 election of Joe Biden and in the 2021 runoff victories of Jon Ossoff and Rev. Raphael Warnock. Vice President Kamala Harris will have a tie-breaking Senate vote.

WARP SPEED WITH SPEED BUMPS

Trump's *Operation Warp Speed* has just stalled.
Our health officials are feeling appalled
At little progress in giving injections
And great alarm at rising infections.
The federal government had no plans
Beyond putting vaccines into states' hands.
Alas, many doses remain on the shelf
Because Donald Trump thought just of himself.
Our states require having more resources,
Perhaps using members of our Armed Forces.
Joe Biden plans an acceleration
To organize the implementation.
  People are anxious, awaiting their turn,
  So longing for normal life to return.

1/15/2021

"Operation Warp Speed" was the Trump administration's slogan for developing effective vaccines to fight the novel coronavirus COVID-19. They deserve praise for achieving that goal in record time. However, vaccine doses sitting in deep freeze or on shelves while COVID rampages across the country is inexcusable. In addition, only 10% of monoclonal antibodies have been administered.

The Trump administration promised 20 million doses given by the end of December. As it stands **on January 16**, only about 11 million persons have received either the Pfizer or Moderna vaccines, which require two injections spaced about a month apart. Johnson and Johnson's vaccine will hopefully be available soon, and one dose is thought to be protective, with sub-freezing storage not required.

DIVISIONS

The checkpoints now scattered throughout D.C.
Remind me of driving through *Checkpoint Charlie.*
In our time in Berlin beside the Wall,
We mourned many deaths before it would fall.
The year we were stationed there, thirty died –
Shot seeking freedom, for orders defied!
It's hard to believe what has happened *here.*
Some may be viewing *our* future with fear.
We must reunite and once more speak truth.
It's vital to teach thinking skills to our youth;
Try hard to erase Trump's poor example.
Repair this breach, and blessings will be ample.
    God bless us and those elected to lead.
    Give thanks that terrorists didn't succeed.

1/16/2021

My husband and I were stationed in West Berlin in 1965. After World War II, Berlin was divided into British, French, American and Russian sectors. Each had barricades and checkpoints. Guards shot on sight persons attempting to flee over the Wall to freedom in West Berlin. We often saw memorials left at the Wall where loved ones had perished. Checkpoint Charlie was the entry or exit point for Americans driving the long corridor through East Germany. Berlin was an "island city" inside Russian-controlled East Germany.

The D.C. checkpoints and hastily erected, tall cyclone fencing topped with razor wire encircle the entire Capitol complex. Preparation is now complete for the open-air inauguration of Joe Biden and Kamala Harris on January 20 at noon. The Capitol Mall is closed to the public, and those attending will be strictly limited. About 25,000 National Guard troops will be in place in D.C. before the swearing-in.

DOG WHISTLE

I heard tonight from Speaker Pelosi
A concept that lately occurred to me.
It explains how crowds swallowed lies they were fed.
"The election was won by Trump," Ted Cruz said.
The underlying message clearly there
For white supremacists with ears to hear,
That huge blocks of Black votes shouldn't be counted,
Although courts turned down all cases mounted.
"Merely a dog whistle," Nancy revealed,
"for white nationalists, barely concealed."
They needed little to rally their cause.
Cries to use violence gave them no pause.
  Will those arrested for their invasion
  Regret their roles on that horrid occasion?

1/19/2021

Speaker of the House Nancy Pelosi was interviewed on MSNBC by Joy Reid for an entire hour tonight.

QAnon leaders are beginning to say, "We all got played" in heeding Trump's call to invade the Capitol Building on January 6 and stop the counting and certification of Electoral College votes. He set them up, indicating he would join them at the Capitol to "fight hard to save their country!" Instead, Trump retreated to the White House where he took great pleasure in viewing on TV the chaos they were creating.

Texas Senator Ted Cruz was one of the main purveyors of lies that the election was stolen from Trump. He spearheaded an effort in the Senate to support the rejection of election results for Biden.

TRANSITION DAY

I felt great relief to see Trump depart,
Emerging from the White House one last time.
His farewell speech held more lies to impart.
He implied the state of the union was fine.
In truth, he left our nation in tatters,
Ravaged by illness and deaths that were tragic.
Biden must deal with many dire matters.
To solve them all would require use of magic.
As dawn broke, I longed for and sensed renewal,
A chance to repair our soiled reputation
After Trump's demand to Pence met refusal.
We're blessed Pence acted with no hesitation.
  Today, I feel hopeful, fully alive.
  I know that our country will again thrive.

1/20/2021

Our fate could have been different if Vice President Mike Pence had followed Trump's directives to substitute different electors who would award *him* the election. Pence did his Constitutional duty.

Inauguration ceremonies were held in front of the U.S. Capitol that was ransacked just two weeks earlier. Twenty-five thousand National Guard troops were stationed in D.C. by Inauguration Day to prevent violence.

I shed a few tears of joy as I watched the arrival of former presidents and spouses, Vice President Mike Pence and his family, Supreme Court justices, leadership of the Senate and House, and family members of the new president and vice president.

INAUGURATION

A few grey clouds and traces of snowflakes
Set the stage for Inauguration Day.
Our civic life is overdue for retakes,
With new direction just installed today.
A burst of bright sun soon broke through the gloom,
Illuminating change now taking place.
Our nation teetered on the edge of doom
When our hallowed Capitol was defaced.
Biden spoke to all of us from his heart.
He pledged transparency, to be truthful.
"Let's listen to each other, make a new start."
We need to unite so change can be useful.
    The insurrection Trump incited failed.
    "Our better angels always have prevailed."

1/20/2021

Joseph R. Biden was installed as 46th President in front of the U.S. Capitol today in a heart-warming and inspiring ceremony. His message was both upbeat and realistic. "My whole soul is in this effort to reunite our country," he said with passion. "Enough of us have come together to carry *all* of us forward."

All the speeches, vocal soloists, the poet laureate's performance, and the address by President Joe Biden were perfection and a true celebration, as our country again embarks on a new, upright path.

The evening celebrations and fireworks were healing – full of hope and inspiration. The world can see, America is back!

ANOTHER COUP AVERTED

A second coup effort was underway
We learned of in the evening news today.
Though not as overt as the D.C. attack,
Success would have set democracy back.
Trump conspired to remove Jeffrey Rosen,
Replacing him with a *toady* he'd chosen
As attorney general in the DOJ.
Jeffrey Clark promised to do things Trump's way.
He asked Clark to void the Georgia election
And elsewhere implement voter rejection.
DOJ attorneys threatened to resign.
Trump rescinded these efforts just in time.
  He'd planned to have the High Court intervene.
  Such corruption here had never been seen.

1/22/2021

When a group of principled attorneys in the Department of Justice threatened to resign en masse, Trump decided to abandon his efforts to delegitimize votes in battleground states in races that had been close.

When this coup attempt did not come to fruition, Trump implemented his final desperate strategy to cling to power. He made an hour-long speech launching the frenzied mob attack on the U.S. Capitol in an attempt to stop the certification of legitimate Electoral College votes.

ANXIETY DREAM

I dreamed I walked into a copy shop
To print out my poetry collection.
At the cashier's desk, a thought made me stop.
I remembered the COVID infection.
Suddenly I felt a shiver of fear.
I had forgotten my mask in the car.
"I would like to leave my printing job here.
I need my mask, and the walk is not far."
I noticed that no one else wore a mask.
Someone grabbed me and sneezed all over me.
Why is wearing a mask too much to ask?
I struggled in vain to break myself free.
  I started to tremble, and then I awoke.
  Protections for COVID-19 are no joke!

1/25/2020

This was an actual dream that I had a few months ago. I wrote a brief piece about it for my Writers' Group. Then I decided also to reflect this unsettling nightmare in a poem. Years ago, I realized that poetry can crystalize thought, conveying emotions and ideas effectively in a small amount of space.

This nightmare occurred shortly before the Thanksgiving holiday, and I was concerned about my daughter's and son's plans for getting together with a few people in "their pod." Those emotions probably triggered my anxiety dream, which was unlike any I'd had before.

I had read about masked peaceful protestors for Black Lives Matter sometimes being accosted by people without masks who opposed their efforts. One woman was seen deliberately *coughing on* demonstrators.

GOING POSTAL!

Our postal system was attacked by DeJoy
Who used every means he could to destroy
The service we needed for our elections,
Especially during COVID infections.
Both DeJoy and Trump schemed to privatize
The Post Office functions we utilize
On a daily basis and found dependable.
Trump had sought to make them expendable.
Lots of sorting machines were dismantled,
Making deliveries poorly handled.
Many drop boxes were taken away,
And often no mail arrived on a weekday.
   Biden must implement reconstruction
   After Trump and DeJoy's mad destruction.

1/29/2021

Louis DeJoy was appointed by Trump to head the U. S. Postal System. He was unqualified, but the political appointee did Trump's bidding. Privatizing the postal system was the ulterior motive. Postal Service employees carried on despite almost impossible conditions, especially during a pandemic. Their dedication and long hours made voting by mail possible and successful. Our nation owes them a great deal!

In addition to the motive to privatize, another strategy was to disrupt the receipt of voting materials and the return of absentee ballots by mail during the 2020 election.

"Going postal" entered our nation's useful phrases in the 1990s. Its use means to become uncontrollably angry, often with violence, and usually in a workplace. Valiant postal workers stayed cool and kept the mail going during these trying times. The Postal System must be repaired!

COVID COMPLICATIONS

We are now seeing COVID mutations
Posing for health experts dire complications
For treatment planning in the months ahead,
And causing once more a feeling of dread.
Just as vaccinations were gaining ground,
Three other lethal variants are found
Invading our country from far-off shores –
England, South Africa, Brazil, and more.
These strains might also be hard to contain.
New vaccines the solution, some maintain.
A booster shot later may be the answer
For those with shots from Moderna or Pfizer.
  Our renowned COVID-19 Task Force team
  Can be trusted to devise a new scheme.

1/29/2021

Just as we were feeling hopeful that we might be able to resume life in our communities again by perhaps next fall, we are faced with new strains of the rapidly mutating coronavirus. Some, like me, have received a first shot from Pfizer or Moderna and are awaiting a second one – if vaccine supplies hold out. Now, we learn we may require a *different* booster shot to protect us from more highly contagious and perhaps more lethal COVID strains.

Most of us elderly folks have become more patient and resilient, knowing that eventually we shall overcome if we follow all the protocols for safety. Revival of the economy is another matter, as is the safe reopening of our schools. These times are especially tough for persons with young children, those in college or recent graduates wanting to begin careers, students who miss sports, performing artists, and small business owners.

THE GREAT DIVIDE

How can we all come together once more
United in spirit from shore to shore
When rancorous feelings mar friendships and kin?
Will we ever see eye to eye again?
Our social ill will goes many years back,
Spoiling relations between white and black,
With sisters and brothers, uncles and aunts,
Worsened by leaders who are sycophants!
A hidden cause may be men's waning power
As the women's movement grows by the hour;
The perceived loss of economic clout;
No desire to learn what *others* are about.
  Our healing can be found by speaking truth,
  Living lives worth emulating by our youth.

1/31/2021

The sycophants I refer to are those who continue to seek the support of disgraced former president, Donald Trump, putting their own prospects for re-election ahead of honor and country. They continue to propagate lies that the election was somehow fraudulent or stolen. Many supporters believe Trump's lies even *months* after the November election results were validated.

A close friend and I both grew up in South Texas and moved to California after living overseas. We are perplexed about our relationships with some of our family members and our former classmates in our home state. The divide continues to be as deep as the Corpus Christi Ship Channel. May we soon find healing!

CONFRONTATION

Biden had a long talk with Vladimir,
Telling him things he long needed to hear.
Donald Trump never had confrontations
On numerous serious occasions
Concerning our nation's security,
Such as having our elections tamper-free.
Joe Biden spoke of bounties on our troops,
Their help defeating Clinton, and other scoops.
He even called out his harming Navalny –
First poisoned, now imprisoned. Set him free!
Cries for his freedom in Russia are surging.
Will there be change after Biden's urging?
    Russian hacking of systems during elections
    Will take time and huge sums to make corrections.

1/31/2021

A positive step, the U.S. and Russia recently renewed our mutual nuclear arms pact, the Start Treaty, set to expire. START I, the most complex arms control treaty in history, removed 80 percent of the strategic nuclear weapons then in existence when proposed by Ronald Reagan. Biden re-opened the door to maintaining the peace between our countries. Yet, he called out Putin for transgressions toward the U.S. during Trump's term of office.

Trump never once stood up to the dictatorial leader of Russia. In truth, he seemed to admire and chose to emulate him. Trump sided with Putin, not our own FBI, in 2016 election meddling charges.

Alexei Navalny, Vladimir Putin's principal opposition leader in Russia, was poisoned with the nerve agent Novichok. Treated in Berlin for five months, he returned to Russia. He was promptly imprisoned.

IMPEACHMENT PREVIEW

A glimpse of Trump's face gives me PTSD
When I think of the harm he caused our country.
Impeachment in the Senate will start soon.
He found no attorneys singing his tune.
A team of five just gave resignations.
In claiming "fraud," they had reservations.
Trump's new legal team defended "the Mob,"
A perfect match for those now on the job.
My hope is that Donald Trump won't appear,
Causing a spectacle, stirring up fear.
May he stay home and watch it on TV,
As he conducted his presidency.
  I pray he'll be forced to pay for his sin.
  Only then can our nation's true healing begin.

2/2/2021

Post traumatic stress disorder develops in some people who have experienced a shocking, scary, or dangerous event. For me, the invasion of our nation's Capitol by unruly and murderous mobs was a PTSD moment. I watched in horror as the attack progressed, and no backup arrived for hours!

The entire Trump presidency is something I would like to permanently erase from my memory.

In all probability, Trump's previous legal team resigned because he was insisting they argue that the election was stolen from him or fraudulent. There is no evidence of fraud or voting irregularities.

COMPETENCE

To me, Joe Biden's positions make sense.
He's putting in place a capable team
Showing a high degree of competence
To deal with issues on our national scene.
Such a contrast in tone Biden is setting
To Donald's inept administration.
It's clear that he and his staff aren't forgetting
The pledges made before inauguration.
The honor and dignity now on display
Have restored my long-lost serenity.
I also sleep well at the end of the day,
Without echoes of actions of insanity.
  I now *look forward* to living my life
  Without feeling dread of the constant strife.

2/2/2021

What a difference two weeks make, even with impeachment ahead. Biden and his team are implementing many changes he promised: on the environment; rejoining our former alliances; tackling thorny immigration issues; reversing policies that pollute air, soil and water; and nationalizing efforts to get large numbers vaccinated for COVID. Regular press briefings with truthful and capable Jen Psaki, as well as COVID Task Force reports with scientists, are rapidly restoring trust from our citizens. Biden also confronted Vladimir Putin about issues that Trump hadn't raised in four years.

Serious efforts are underway to get a $1.9 billion COVID relief package passed in Congress to revive our struggling economy and give assistance to those most in need.

CAPITOL POLICE HERO HONORED

The cremains of a hero lie in state
In the D.C. Capitol where he served.
He died defending those who legislate.
His murder was not a fate he deserved.
For twelve years he faithfully guarded his post,
Always with a happy heart and a smile.
Brian was among those admired the most.
He was honored as they passed single file.
Brian Sicknick succumbed at forty-two,
Bludgeoned by thugs in the D.C. attack.
'Though outnumbered, to his oath he stayed true.
He died with his integrity intact.
   Brian Sicknick lies with honor today.
   He gave up his life in a valiant way.

2/3/2021

Capitol Police Officer Brian Sicknick, 42, is only the fifth private citizen to lie under the Capitol Rotunda Dome in our nation's history. His burial will take place today with honors at Arlington National Cemetery.

The correct term for Sicknick's commemoration is that he lies under the Capitol Rotunda in *honor*.

Last night and this morning, our nation's leaders of both parties came to pay their respects, along with other officers serving with the Capitol Police. His parents and two brothers were present to observe the solemn and dignified ritual.

SPEAKING OUT

I must speak out; I cannot be tongue-tied.
The truth as I see it won't be denied.
Since the day after Trump was elected,
I made it my goal to see him rejected.
I never fathomed that threats to democracy
Might quickly result in autocracy.
Shame on Congressmen there on January sixth,
Yet voted that our election was fixed!
It baffles me that more people can't see
How our prized form of law is in jeopardy.
'Though Trump's *next* impeachment may also fail,
There's no doubt in my mind, he belongs in jail!
  Impeachment proceedings may bring more to light,
  Causing more persons to embrace what is right.

2/3/2021

The impeachment proceedings that begin next week will be the *second time* Trump has been impeached for his one term of office. Defenders will try to argue "process," that you can't remove a president already out of office. Mitch McConnell refused to call the Senate back into session in urgent fashion. Therefore, trial in the Senate was delayed to the second week in February. The House sent its one article of impeachment to the Senate promptly after the Capitol insurrection on January 6th, while Trump was still in office. No one is above the law or should be given a free pass due to technicalities, especially after such a flagrant attempt to take over our government in unlawful fashion.

SERVING ABROAD

Joe Biden addressed foreign service workers.
Diplomats and envoys are not shirkers.
With close ties to allies again allowed,
Their service to our nation will make us proud.
"You're the face of America that others see.
Diplomacy is back, with integrity.
I believe in you and will have your back.
The world will see we are once more on track.
You are the center of what we must do.
Our esteem and support will travel with you.
The work is enormous, with trust to regain.
We'll uphold human rights worldwide again."
  For four years our values were disregarded.
  We must show the world they can't be discarded.

2/4/2021

President Joseph Biden addressed today a new class of foreign service workers. Their ranks had been drastically thinned by Trump's failure to make new appointments and due to retirements by the disillusioned. He emphasized his belief that we are now better equipped to defend other democracies because we have (recently) fought for it ourselves.

While in the U.S. Senate, Joe Biden served as chairman of the Foreign Relations Committee for many years. He has more experience in foreign policy than any previous president.

Foreign service diplomats, envoys, ambassadors and other workers make great sacrifices to serve their country abroad. They uproot their families and often serve in dangerous posts around the world.

DEFRAGGING

My sleeping brain, I think, is defragging –
Deleting old stuff – it seems to be lagging.
The past four years have seen so much to store,
But I do not want it there anymore.
My brain may protest in the week ahead.
I'll set aside work, watch *impeachment* instead.
Though not present, Trump will be center stage,
Sparing us the spectacle of his rage.
Why will not "the Donald" himself appear?
Self-incrimination, his attorneys fear.
How blissful I've felt, not seeing his face.
Most of his rantings, I'd like to erase.
   Watching the process will be compelling,
   With swarms of armed insurgents rebelling.

2/6/2021

The impeachment managers will present incriminating videos taken on January 6th of the incitement to riot by Trump, his family members, and Attorney Rudy Giuliani. They also have a treasure trove of videos and photos from the actual invasion of the Capitol. Facebook posts and tweets by glory-seeking participants add more evidence of breaking and entering, physical violence that led to serious injuries and deaths, and the mob's shouts to "Hang Mike Pence" and shoot Speaker of the House Nancy Pelosi. They will also present evidence from Trump's "hostage video" message that he finally was compelled to deliver. In addressing the violent mob, he told them that he "loved them," they should always remember that day, but that they must "return home in peace." For hours he had gleefully watched their rampages on TV from the White House. Trump never tried to intervene or call more law enforcement to back up vastly outnumbered Capitol Police.

Defragging means defragmenting to make a computer run better.

SEPARATIONS AND REUNIFICATIONS

A policy of Trump's has made me cry,
Dividing families at our border.
Few asked to enforce it dared to defy.
Grabbing children, just following an order.
Many had walked countless miles to flee death,
Seeking safety in the "Land of the Free."
Their arrival left them feeling bereft.
They found separation, not sanctuary.
Even nursing babies were snatched away
With no system or plan to reunite.
Deported across the border to stay,
Frantic parents didn't know how to fight.
  Biden has started reunification
  For families enduring separation.

2/8/2021

These Donald Trump policies, intended to deter illegal immigration and encourage tougher legislation, were in place from 2017 until June 2018. As a result of these heartless policies, it is thought that between 650 and 2,000 families are still seeking reunification. In many cases, it will be impossible to find parents or guardians deported to Mexico or Central America without their children. As many as 5,000 children may have been taken from their families.

I remember vividly a media account of a father shooting himself in the head soon after his young son was ripped from his arms. I cried!

At this juncture, the Biden administration is beginning a painstaking process of trying to locate parents and reunite them with their children. About nine families have been tearfully reunited thus far.

DANGER LURKING

Nine-Eleven and One-Six, each a tragic date,
Events to which all of us can relate.
The first hellish day brought us together,
While the second caused relations to sever.
Impeachment is on, with reactions mixed.
Stark videos in our minds are now fixed.
The vote today sends Trump's case to trial.
Attorney Castor is not in denial.
He admitted aloud that Biden won.
Castor may be fired, though he'd just begun.
In case of acquittal, what will Trump do?
Will he try to stir up another coup?
  I hope our leaders are prepared to act
  If insurrectionists again attack!

2/9/2021

Lead attorney for Trump's defense is Bruce Castor, whose argument was that Congress didn't need to impeach him. Americans had just voted to replace an out of favor president. The remedy is to *arrest him* if he is guilty of crimes. That comment must have enraged Trump!

Impeachment managers for Democrats are showing disturbing video clips of the Capitol invasion, along with timelines vividly illustrating that for hours, Trump never tried to stop the violence. In fact, he continued to tweet more incitement to the mob as the riot progressed.

Terrorists now communicate with messages that are more hidden and using encryption, making it difficult to uncover their plans in advance.

GOOD MAN GOODMAN

Officer Goodman lived up to his name.
Defending the Capitol earned him fame.
He bravely deflected the crazed insurgents
By taking smart actions as diversions.
He lured them away from the Senate's hall.
Quick thinking and actions had saved them all
As Senators and staffers slipped away,
Evacuated down the vacant hallway.
He modestly didn't seek recognition;
Just acting in his policeman position.
His family's safety entered his mind,
Not wanting them in a dangerous bind.
  A medal of gold has been awarded
  To honor him for the mayhem thwarted.

2/10/2021

Capitol Police Officer Eugene Goodman was concerned for the lives of his wife and children. The valiant Black man and his family had received death threats from Trump supporters. The attack on the Capitol was primarily led by white supremacist groups.

A Senate resolution was introduced in mid-January to award Officer Goodman a Congressional Gold Medal. It was unanimously approved. Republican Senator Thom Tillis remarked, "Facing down a mob of rioters, Officer Goodman led the violent mob away from the Senate floor where they were mere feet away from Senators and the Vice President, Mike Pence. I stand with colleagues in our gratitude for his heroic actions. I'm honored to co-introduce this bipartisan legislation."

LOVE OF COUNTRY

I feel an ardent love of my country,
Passed on by my immigrant dad to me.
He arrived in New York in 1905
To work with cousins, with faith he could thrive.
His dreams were fulfilled in our bountiful land.
He gave back in serving when there was demand.
Carl volunteered for duty in Eastern France
In World War I, with the Allies' advance.
Today, when I see our republic at stake,
I ponder what course our nation will take.
My love for this country has never been stronger.
May it flourish for centuries longer!
  True democracies in this world are rare.
  We must protect and defend ours with care.

2/12/2021

My father, Carl Henny, immigrated to the U.S. from Holland in 1905 when he was 17. Too young to become a citizen, he was called back in 1908 to serve a year in the Dutch Army. Not responding would have made him "a man without a country." Years later, he proudly took the oath to become a U.S. citizen.

During World War I, my dad volunteered for hazardous duty. He was sent to France near Metz, where he directed detonations of artillery shells. His service in the U.S. Army occurred at the height of the 1918 "Spanish Flu." That pandemic swept across the globe, taking huge casualties among armed forces. I am grateful that both Carl and my mother, Amelia (age 18 in San Antonio), survived. They had not yet met. Neither parent ever mentioned the Spanish Flu pandemic. I was unaware of it until its centennial in 2018 when an article appeared in *Smithsonian* magazine.

ACQUITTAL

The impeachment verdict was predicted,
That Donald Trump wouldn't be convicted.
Republicans shirked responsibility,
Hiding behind a technicality.
Their outrage should have carried the day.
Instead, most cast votes under Mitch's sway.
Seven courageously strayed from the pack.
These patriots now have targets on their back.
House managers skillfully proved their case,
But forty-three thought of their next campaign race.
The threat of mob actions will not fade away.
I fear homegrown factions are here to stay.
   After the acquittal, Mitch made harsh remarks.
   He should have tried to prevent future sparks.

2/13/2021

The vote was 57-43 to impeach Trump. It fell 10 votes short of a two-thirds majority needed to impeach the 45th president. It was the largest bi-partisan majority voting to convict in our history.

After voting, Mitch McConnell delivered a scathing rebuke of Trump on his incitement to violence and dereliction of duty in not intervening to halt the attack on the Capitol on January 6, 2021. He hid behind the false stipulation that a president out of office cannot be impeached, even for crimes committed while still in office and with the process initiated before his term ended. McConnell refused to call the Senate back into session to deal with the urgent matter while Trump was still in office. This concept had been proven false in earlier legal arguments of constitutionality. This dangerous precedent would allow a "January exception" for a future corrupt president to use with *weeks left* in office.

WINNERS

The impeachment managers from the House,
A spell-binding team that was well prepared,
All won their compelling case, there's no doubt,
But most Republicans were running scared.
It's strange how some who shrank from a YES vote
Now are following Mitch McConnell's lead.
May their party's base observe and take note.
Some are now condemning Trump's vilest deed.
The stellar team for the prosecution
Represented the complexions of our land.
The defense could not match their elocution.
They must have desired to vacate the stand.
  Impeachment managers can take great pride;
  Their praises are echoing far and wide.

2/15/2021

Shortly after the impeachment vote was taken and Trump was acquitted, Minority Leader of the Senate Mitch McConnell delivered a strong rebuke of the former president's criminal behavior: "Trump is still criminally liable for everything he did in office," he said. "He didn't get away with anything YET! He is now subject to criminal justice and civil litigation for which he can be liable until statutes of limitations run out."

President Trump's vilest deed, and the action for which he was impeached, was the incitement of the attack on the U.S. Capitol and the attempt to stop the counting of electoral votes. Seven Republicans voted with Democrats to convict, but the effort fell ten votes short of the two-thirds majority needed.

All impeachment managers were magnificent. They represented diversity that makes our country great! Lead manager was Jamie Raskin, D-MD.

TURMOIL

Once more, I can't seem to sleep through the night.
The moments of harmony seemed too brief.
Impeachment stoked the political fight.
Trump's lingering influence gives us grief.
Democrats had no choice but to proceed
After that foul deed against our nation.
Yet, Congress must act when there is great need,
When many among us feel desperation.
Speaker Pelosi proposed a commission
To investigate the Capitol's breach,
While they try to move on with Biden's transition.
He may address this topic in a speech.
  How does our president manage his stress?
  None before him inherited such a mess!

2/16/2021

The attack on the U.S. Capitol on January 6, 2021 was directed by Donald J. Trump as he attempted to remain in office as president despite losing the election to Joe Biden. The ONE impeachment article dealt with this tragedy and the stain on our democracy.

The COVID-19 Relief Bill must be passed soon to give suffering lower income Americans economic relief, and to provide additional funding for vaccines and vital government services. Our coronavirus problem is still silently lurking, with over 488,000 deaths and 29 million infected.

Yesterday, Speaker of the House Nancy Pelosi (D-CA), voiced a need for a 9-11 style bipartisan commission to look into the breach of the Capitol by marauders. Investigations may take a year.

AMONG THE LUCKY

A month ago, I traveled to Kaiser
Where I received my first dose from Pfizer.
That day was already a joyful one,
The Wednesday Joe Biden's term had begun.
"I feel I've won the lottery today,"
I overheard another patient say.
We rejoiced, while under brief observation,
To be among the first in the nation.
All of us were over seventy-five
And trying our darndest to stay alive.
Last Thursday, I received my second shot.
'Though vaccinated, I'll act like I'm not.
  Two weeks are needed to build immunity.
  I will protect myself and community.

2/17/2021

On Wednesday, January 20, 2021, Trump left the White House and Joe Biden was inaugurated. What a happy day it was, all around. The vaccine rollouts have been slow due to scant quantities of vaccine and poor organization from the Trump administration. Now, severe winter weather is grounding flights and causing the disruption of vaccine supplies. Some are having their vaccinations postponed, after great difficulty in scheduling an appointment.

Today, my daughter sent me an article stating that European DNA containing traces of Neanderthal genes can be beneficial to persons with that genetic makeup. It is thought to protect them from the most severe cases of COVID-19. I learned from *Twenty-three and Me* that I have a reasonably high component of Neanderthal DNA. Bless those Neanderthals, who once lived in Northern Europe.

TEXAS: HELL FROZEN OVER

People are freezing; there's nothing to eat.
They have no reliable source of heat.
Their pipes are bursting and toilets won't flush.
Ice and snow on the ground hasn't turned to slush.
Some folks are ill or aged and alone.
Outside contact is spotty by cellphone.
Stores have scant stocks of food and bottled water.
People may soon be required to barter.
Some families are sleeping in their car,
But gasoline is hard to find, near or far.
Everyone is bundling up to stay warm,
While more Arctic blasts may soon cause more harm.
  In this sad time, when COVID is looming
  Ways to connect are few without *Zooming*.

2/18/2021

This most recent disaster in Texas is related to climate change, as the polar vortex dips further south. Oklahoma was colder than Texas but had no problems, as they are on a national power grid, where power sharing is possible. The Lone Star State had chosen to ignore warnings from FERC – after similar power grid emergencies in 1989 and 2011 – that they must winterize their energy producing and delivery systems. Texas also opted to utilize a stand-alone energy grid system (ERCOT), not wanting any government regulation or interference in their energy production. It works well and is lucrative until an Arctic front such as this one sweeps through and spreads misery everywhere across the state. Texas came close to having the entire grid crash. All energy production systems failed, and pipes breaking or cracking caused extensive damage to property, as well as making water unsafe to drink in many places. Some with a fireplace were burning furniture to stay warm.

PROFILE IN COURAGE

Jamie Raskin is a profile in courage,
Whose son's tragic death didn't discourage
From his serving as lead prosecution
In the Senate with flawless execution.
They laid Tom to rest January 5.
The next day, his family barely survived
The Capitol attack, hiding in fear
While marauders could be heard passing near.
Tommy, 25, was his middle child,
A brilliant law student, but his demons beguiled.
He took his own life; left an apology.
He'd long battled his dark psychology.
  Raskin recited words of Thomas Paine,
  The person for whom his son had been named:

2/19/2021

"His depression was a kind of relentless torture in the brain for him. Despite very fine doctors and a loving family...the pain became overwhelming, unyielding and unbearable at last." **Rep. Raskin, D-MD**

Tom's suicide note said: **"Please forgive me. My illness won today..."**

"These are the times that try men's souls. The summer soldier and the sunshine patriot will, in this crisis, shrink from service of their country; but he that stands it now, deserves the love and thanks of man and woman. Tyranny ... is not easily conquered; yet ... the harder the conflict, the more glorious the triumph..." **(T.Paine)**

Rep. Raskin said he told his daughter her next visit there would be different. Her poignant response: "Dad, I don't want to come back to the Capitol."

ANTI-ASIAN TRAUMA

Attacks on Asians are on the increase.
What will it take to cause them to cease?
For a whole year we had heard Trump exclaim,
"The Chinese Virus; China is to blame!"
He also expressed it as "the Kung Flu."
Those prejudiced words can incite a few.
Old men are forcefully shoved with disdain.
One Asian was slashed while riding a train.
Another fell, hit his head hard and died.
Most assailants are not identified.
How can we stop these assaults and robberies
Occurring most often against Chinese?
  We must devote more police resources.
  Also, speak out in a chorus of voices.

2/20/2021

I live in a beautiful neighborhood where people of all races live together in harmony. Several good friends on my block are Chinese. It pains me to read about and see on television that crimes against Asians have increased by 150 percent in the past year.

Before the pandemic, Chinatown in Oakland and San Francisco were thriving. They were exciting places to visit for their food markets, terrific restaurants, and Chinese New Year parades. May they again be safe, economically viable, and enjoyable for people of all races.

If you should hear a racial slur against any race, speak out and show your strong disapproval.

HIGHER EDUCATION

Community college should be cost-free,
The best tonic for our democracy.
More education is being required.
For better jobs, it's needed to be hired.
Strange conspiracies are widely believed.
More schooling could result in fewer deceived.
With society much more complex today,
A need for more learning is here to stay.
When QAnon believers taint our House
It's hard to fathom theories they espouse.
Standards should be met to run for Congress.
We need those with qualities that impress.
  Ability to pay shouldn't hold youths back.
  More education would provide skills they lack.

2/21/2021

President Joe Biden has repeatedly emphasized that free education should be provided by our community colleges.

I find it hard to understand how a candidate such as Rep. Marjorie Taylor Greene was elected from Georgia to serve in the U.S. House of Representatives. She is known to have swallowed the insane conspiracy theories of QAnon and even propagated them. She also suggested that Speaker of the House Nancy Pelosi should get a bullet to her head. Greene has tried to evade newly installed metal detectors at the Capitol. Hefty fines will now be imposed for doing so. Pelosi and Rep. Alexandria Occasio Cortez have both decried the "enemy within" the sacred halls of Congress.

Marjorie Taylor Greene was recently removed from the Education Committee, but Republicans refused to expel or roundly condemn her.

COMPLIANCE

For COVID prevention, I'm in compliance.
I don't understand why some show defiance.
So many won't mask or take the vaccine
After five hundred thousand deaths we've seen.
Tomorrow will count as my fourteenth day
Since my second shot, I'm happy to say.
In my wallet, I have a card to show
That I've had both shots, so others will know.
I pray that new variants won't complicate
As new strains continue to replicate.
I trust that scientists will have the skill
To eradicate COVID by shot or pill.
  Until the day when COVID is no threat
  I'll do what I can to see guidelines are met.

2/24/2021

As of today, the COVID-19 death toll in the U.S. alone is **506,000**. With only four percent of the world's population, our country has about twenty-five percent of COVID fatalities. America first, indeed! (*America First!* was Trump's slogan that guided international policies.)

Brief memorial services have been held this week as we remember and honor those who died of coronavirus. Our casualties from COVID are higher than combined U.S. fatalities in World War I, World War II, and Vietnam.

ENDURANCE

That year began with feeling so alone.
Yet, meeting each crisis, I think I've grown.
When suddenly compelled to isolate,
I felt inadequate, bemoaned my fate.
'Though I've not seen my family all year,
On Zoom, they speak and magically appear.
I order groceries with Instacart.
Our writers' meetings are still heart to heart.
I've lived through power loss and deadly smoke,
With air outside that makes me cough and choke;
Through home upgrades and needed renovations;
The worst, dreading quick evacuations.
  Since COVID broke out, I've not just survived;
  It's possible that in some ways I've thrived.

2/25/2021

I'm referring to the beginning of 2020, when COVID-19 first appeared in California. I last saw my son and daughter in person in January that year, and my grandkids in November of 2019. Sheltering in place began in California in mid-March of 2020. At that time, I wrote my first COVID-19 sonnet that I called *Coronavirus Lament*. Its tone was dark and desperate.

We had the worst air quality in the world for several weeks, with wildfires raging north, south, and east of us. I rarely ventured out, and I wore an N-95 mask if it was urgent to go outside. I learned my lesson the year before when I came down with a bad case of bronchitis after walking in smoky air.

Virtual writers' meetings and church services are valuable connections until we can be together face to face once more.

COVID-19 MILESTONES

In just one year, half a million have died
And *more,* with the cause unidentified.
In the early days, some expired at home
When little about the virus was known.
At COVID's debut, we had scant testing
Or knowledge of how it was infesting.
Today, we're fully informed on its spread,
And with vaccines, people are feeling less dread.
Just fifteen percent have been vaccinated
But a third vaccine now is celebrated.
Johnson & Johnson needs only one shot,
And they'll quickly ramp up the doses they've got.
  The new vaccine doesn't need deep freezing
  The significance, requirements are easing.

3/1/2021

The first official U.S. death from COVID-19 took place on February 29, 2020. I believe many cases here were *under the radar* in the early days. More than 513,000 have now died.

President Donald Trump had been briefed in January 2020 about the lethality and methods of spread, but he chose to conceal that information, saying he didn't want to "cause a panic." He admitted this fact in a taped interview with author Bob Woodward, for his second book about Trump.

The three vaccines approved are from Pfizer, Moderna, and Johnson & Johnson. All are highly effective and prevent serious illness, hospitalization and death from COVID-19. J&J is much easier to store and transport.

IDOLATRY

The conference held by CPAC this week
Where Republican conservatives met
To promote their causes and hear Trump speak
Was a love fest groupies won't soon forget.
A garish statue of their idol was raised,
It's metallic face resembling gold,
While videos and speakers showered praise
For the speaker they waited to behold.
After much fanfare, Trump mounted the stage.
He repeated lies about the election.
When speaking of Biden, he was filled with rage.
It seemed few attendees thought of defection.
  Trump and his worshipers pose a grave threat.
  Sadly, we've not seen the last of him yet!

3/2/2021

The Conservative Political Action Conference (CPAC) is an annual political conference attended by conservative activists and elected officials from across the United States. CPAC is hosted by the American Conservative Union (ACU).

The most egregious thing Trump did was to call out *by name* all Republicans who voted against him recently, namely to condemn the incitement of violence at the Capitol and those who voted for impeachment. He will do all he can to see those more moderate Republicans defeated when they run in primaries. Worst of all, he endangers them and their families who are already getting death threats for their political stances. Some are afraid to oppose him.

LEADERSHIP

Joe Biden announced a breakthrough today.
Invoking the Defense Production Act,
He made a deal with Merck and J&J.
These two competitors signed a contract.
Merck will help turn out J&J's vaccine,
Enough for all adults to be protected.
They'll work night and day in the best effort seen.
By mid-June, we'll have fewer infected.
Biden has plans to re-open all schools.
Teachers and staff will be vaccine-prioritized.
Pre-K through 12 workers will then have tools
To safely open, with schools sanitized.
These steps are bold, exactly what's needed
To see COVID-19 at last defeated.

3/3/2021

Two of the largest pharmaceutical-producing companies that are also big competitors have come together to perform as a team. By working 24/7, they can produce by the end of May enough of the Johnson & Johnson vaccine for all adults in the U.S. who choose to receive the one-shot dose. This cooperative venture should move the vaccination process forward by at least two months.

Within the next few weeks, teachers and support staff should be able to get vaccinated at their local pharmacy. With most adults who work in Pre-K through 12 protected, and with other precautions, schools should soon be safe for re-opening. After a year of isolation, many students are losing ground and having mental health issues.

CLUELESS

As deaths approach tolls of our Civil War,
They exceed other countries' losses, by far.
Much needless suffering here has been seen.
Trump's denial and inaction were obscene.
Joe Biden's smart policies could stop the spread
Of COVID-19, still filling us with dread.
Supplies of vaccine are expanding soon.
We *might* see good progress by early June.
Yet, clueless governors set efforts back.
Leaders in some states are under attack
For lately discouraging wearing a mask;
No business restrictions that doctors ask.
  Our nation is close to reaching our goal.
  Why would we now dig a much deeper hole?

3/6/2021

Unless we continue to follow the guidelines scrupulously, new and constantly mutating variants may render our current vaccines ineffective. Vaccinations are just gaining ground, with two million doses given a day. In the U.S., 1,500 people are still dying of COVID daily. The death toll today is 524,000. Our Civil War toll: 618,000.

President Joe Biden called out Republican Gov. Greg Abbott for his recent directive to open all businesses in Texas and his stating that masks were no longer needed. The governor of Mississippi, also a Republican, made similar calls to action, dismissing the lingering threat of COVID-19. Alabama may follow suit in April, according to the Republican governor of that state. Spring break is looming, and young people tired of restrictions may set aside caution and flock to popular southern beaches.

AMERICAN RESCUE PLAN

The COVID-19 Relief Bill has passed,
Providing most things that Democrats asked.
No Republicans voted for the bill
Which passed in the Senate with Chuck Schumer's skill.
They endured a tedious all-night session
To forge a bill without major concession.
"You delivered what our country most needed."
For Republicans, their public wasn't heeded.
With food lines and many facing eviction,
How could a NO vote be cast with conviction?
Funds are for the jobless and to re-open schools.
Those opposed were in line with McConnell's rules.
"We're fighting hard to improve people's lives
And to see that our country once more thrives."

3/6/2021

An enthusiastic Joe Biden made comments on Saturday, March 6. He expects to sign the bill on Thursday, March 11, after the lightly amended legislation is again passed in the House. "This bill is a giant step forward. It will make it possible to cut child poverty in half. We want to give everyone a fighting chance and to make a difference in their lives," he said.

The $1.9 trillion COVID Relief Plan passed by a 50-49 vote in the Senate. It contains $1,400 stimulus checks for lower income groups; weekly $300 jobless benefits through September 6, 2021; state and local government assistance; school reopening funds; relief for renters and landlords and small businesses; and money for COVID vaccines and delivery into people's arms, among other things.

SOULS TO THE POLLS

Some states are proposing voting restrictions.
The GOP loses with strong voter turnout.
The party acts on their basest convictions,
Aiming to create suppression and doubt.
In Georgia, proposals are quite severe,
Requiring IDs to vote absentee.
No Sunday "Souls to the Polls" Blacks revere;
To vote by mail would require disability,
Age sixty-five plus, or to be out of town.
For some small infractions, imposing of fines;
Curtail early voting and drop boxes around;
A crime to give water to those in long lines.
  Democracy depends on fair voting rights
  Unrestricted by these political fights.

3/9/2021

It's disgusting what Republicans are doing in Georgia and other battleground states. The House passed HR-1 and sent it to the Senate. That important voting rights legislation must pass in the evenly split Senate and be signed into law by President Joe Biden. This bill would protect and standardize the election procedures across the nation, making voting processes fair and accessible to all eligible voters.

There are currently 253 bills circulating in 43 states that seek to restrict access to voting, especially for Black and brown communities. Most of these states are attempting to end weekend voting. If passed, those changes would have enormous consequences for minorities who must work on weekdays and depend upon weekend voting or absentee ballots to cast votes. *Souls to the Polls* is sponsored by Black churches. Congregations walk together or take a bus to the polls after services.

BUILDING CONSENSUS

One could clearly see the joy and the pride
On Chuck Schumer's face on cable TV.
What Democrats achieved can't be denied.
The diverse party showed rare unity.
"We can get things done to make lives better;
The public will see help is on the way!"
The Rescue Act passed almost to the letter
In the House where the bill returned today.
Biden praised Schumer's working so skillfully.
"He has ably brought his party around
As a leader who worked so patiently."
Broad support from the public can be found.
    In the year since *pandemic* was declared,
    We have good reason to become less scared.

3/10/2021

Chuck Schumer was hiding in the Capitol on January 6th during the insurrection incited by Trump when the New York Democrat learned he would become Senate Majority Leader. His life was spared due to quick actions of the Capitol Police. Scores of invaders were searching for "the Big Jew" that day.

President Biden highly praised Chuck Schumer's work as the new Senate majority leader, saying that in his 38 years in the Senate, he had rarely seen such effective leadership.

One year ago, the World Health Organization declared a global COVID-19 pandemic. Harsh restrictions were put in place, during which many began sheltering in place at home.

FIRST PRIME TIME ADDRESS

"The most American thing that we do
Is finding light in the darkness and gloom."
In this year of job losses, with prospects few,
Folks are homeless, hungry, with feelings of doom.
Too many have died, and often alone.
We miss the events that filled us with joy
And ceremonies we've had to postpone.
Take heart! We have vaccines we can employ.
Now is the time we must come together,
Observing precautions health experts advise;
One nation, one people who care for each other.
We can vanquish COVID if actions are wise.
  The sun will soon rise on a brighter day
  When our bitter tears will be wiped away.

3/11/2021

President Biden's first prime time address was a message of hope, empathy, and conciliation, while also acknowledging the pain each of us has endured during this year-long emergency. "I carry a card in my pocket. Today, the COVID death toll in our country is 527,726."

He urged us to "tell the truth; follow science, and have faith in our government. Government is We the People. It's all of us! There is nothing we can't do when we do it together!"

The president emphasized progress being made in vaccines given and the expanding places where shots are available. "Millions of grandparents can now hug their grandkids. Get your vaccination when it is your turn, and also help your neighbors to get theirs. By July 4th, we may be able to have small groups in backyard BBQs, but with new variants, conditions may change. Listen to Dr. Fauci."

MARS ROVER

The *Perseverance* made a safe Mars landing,
Traveling nearly 300 million miles.
The engineering feat was outstanding!
At Mission Control, loud shouts and broad smiles.
The NASA feat showed the ingenuity
Of our scientists in space exploration.
Little is beyond possibility
With their brainpower and dedication.
Thousands of people took part in the mission
In this pivotal moment for the U.S.
Were there once life forms, as we envision?
Can a manned expedition one day meet success?
  Perseverance is NASAs ninth landing on Mars
  With this rover the largest, most complex of "cars."

3/12/2021

The flawless Mars landing marked the ninth by the U.S., with NASA's fifth and largest rover. It weighs over a metric ton. The perfect descent avoided all the hazards in a place on Mars never before visited. The ancient lakebed and river delta may show signs life once existed there. The sophisticated rover will extract rocks, and a manned expedition in about a decade can transport them to Earth. It will search for fossilized microbes in the lakebed. The vehicle will traverse about 15 miles over the next two years at 0.1 miles per hour. It carries a small helicopter and also instruments that will attempt to convert the Martian carbon dioxide into oxygen. These experiments will help NASA scientists learn to produce rocket fuel on Mars, and potentially oxygen needed in future human exploration of the red planet. The teams overcame challenges of preparing *Perseverance* during COVID-19. The rover left Earth over six months ago.

SPRING BREAKERS

Spring breakers may set us far back, I fear,
After making good progress this past year.
I understand their pent-up emotion,
Their strong desire to be near the ocean.
A third wave is cresting across the sea;
New variants are causing more misery.
How can we protect from the looming threat
When many have not been vaccinated yet?
Most revelers decline to wear a mask
Or keep their distance as health experts ask.
They are mingling closely indoors at night.
The young appear to be *immune* to fright!
   Be wary of bars, link-ups with a stranger;
   Keep yourself and family out of danger.

3/16/2021

The British variant B.1.1.7 is known to be present in Florida and Texas, where many spring breakers are mixing and mingling on beaches and inside bars, cafes and nightclubs. Most are not observing guidelines to protect from COVID-19. Spring break is likely to be a super-spreader event, with new virus waves extending across the U.S. after the revelers disperse and return to their own communities. This variant appears to spread more quickly than previous strains of COVID.

Some European countries are having to lock down again, after new variants wreaked havoc on their communities. At this point, our vaccines appear to be effective against the U.K. variant.

STOP THE HATE!

Atlanta's shootings could have been foreseen,
When Donald Trump continued to demean
Our Asian neighbors living in our midst,
Making racial slurs he could not resist.
The *hatred virus* continued to grow.
Its virulence affected those we know
Who now are frightened for their next of kin.
The threats are real from *the enemy within*.
This week, eight were murdered in Asian spas
By a creep who shot them all without cause.
He tried to blame it on sex addiction,
But racial hatred was his affliction.
  We must stand up for our sisters and brothers
  To stop this violence on Asian *others*.

3/20/2021

Six of the eight people shot at close range by a 21-year-old white male were women of Asian descent. One of the eight victims was a man. The three Atlanta massage parlors' names indicated Asian operation. This recent atrocity could have been an outgrowth of Trump's year-long pandemic-fueled racist attacks against Asians. There have been 3,795 reported anti-Asian incidents since the pandemic broke out.

President Biden and Vice President Harris visited Atlanta, Georgia and spoke out against this insidious hate crime. According to Harris – whose mother was South Asian – xenophobia, misogyny and sexism are real in America. Part of the problem is the hyper-sexualization of Asian women. The perpetrator looked at the victims, not as people, but as symptoms of his sex addiction illness, she said. I will not name him here.

CODE BREAKERS

Jennifer Doudna and a French colleague
Were jointly awarded a Nobel Prize.
Their mRNA advances allowed "Warp Speed"
To fight COVID, a feat no one denies.
The complex science behind the vaccine
Was developed more than ten years ago.
In only two days, the fastest time seen,
Moderna's formula was ready to go.
With each mutation, new boosters can be made
To come up with an updated answer.
With CRISPR gene editing, science can aid
Fighting virus, flawed genetics and cancer.
  Moral and political quandries may loom,
  But CRISPR's current uses are a boon.

3/21/2021

Dr. Jennifer Doudna is an American biochemist known for her pioneering work in CRISPR gene editing, for which she and her French colleague, Emmanuelle Charpentier, received the 2020 Nobel Prize in Chemistry. Dr. Doudna and several other leading biologists called for a worldwide ban on any clinical application of gene editing using CRISPR. She supports using the technology in somatic gene editing, involving alterations not passed to the next generation, but opposes germline gene editing to deliberately change the human race.

Walter Isaacson has profiled Jennifer Doudna for her huge impact on the scientific community in his most recent book, ***The Code Breaker, The Future of the Human Race***. He praises the potential to edit our genes to prevent genetic diseases, but also envisions moral and geopolitical pitfalls in the life-saving technologies. According to Isaacson, "The pandemic changed my thinking."

SORROW

We are sensitized to reports of death.
Millions from COVID took their last breath.
We might accept those as "natural cause,"
But random gun violence gives us pause.
In our Senate, many choose to defy
While the innocent continue to die
From gruesome weapons intended for war
By gunmen with actions known as bizarre.
In Boulder, Colorado, ten were slain.
A second mass shooting this week is insane!
We must enact measures for gun control
To put an end to this terrible toll.
  Eric Talley's seven children have no dad.
  Our nation is mourning, collectively sad.

3/23/2021

The first mass shooting took place in Atlanta, Georgia on March 16. Eight people, six of Asian ethnicity, were killed at three spas.

In this most recent atrocity, ten people between the ages of 20 and 64 were slain inside a grocery store. The first policeman at the scene, **Eric Talley**, was killed on March 22 by a 21-year-old gunman who bought his assault rifle a week earlier. He was shot in the leg and taken into custody. Officer Talley, age 51, leaves a wife and seven children to grieve their great loss.

These tragedies are revitalizing efforts to re-introduce legislation banning assault weapons, requiring background checks for all gun sales, and other measures to curtail mass shootings in the U.S. About 82 percent of the public favors these restrictions. We must rid our society of easy access to weapons of war to keep ourselves and our loved ones safe.

REUNION

My heart was overflowing with gladness
With vaccines helping to end my sadness.
I hugged my two grandchildren, grown so tall.
We last met in 2019 in fall.
Little Mia, always lithe and limber
And Will, precocious as I remember.
They are thriving, despite remote learning.
Seeing my daughter fulfilled my yearning.
One day, COVID will silently retreat.
Getting vaccines in arms, an amazing feat.
We must help create mass immunity
To restore our broken community.
We can't yet relax all cautious protections
'Till more get vaccines to stop infections.

3/24/2021

We three family members of the older generation have had both shots, and my daughter has had one, with her second this week. I rejoiced when I heard that fully vaccinated older folks could now hug their grandchildren. I took them at their word. We still followed protocols recommended, wearing masks and meeting together in the open air. We had two tables at dinnertime, one for the fully vaccinated and another for my daughter, her husband, and the two grandkids. It was truly a happy and long-awaited event!

I'm hoping that more anti-vaccine folks will come around so that we can more quickly develop herd immunity and vanquish COVID. About 15 percent of adults in the U.S. are fully vaccinated and 27 percent had one shot. Vaccine testing in children is now beginning.

FIRST NEWS CONFERENCE: A CONTRAST

Biden's first press event was civilized
With no dodging of questions, insults or lies.
He outlined his major priorities
While praising the leading authorities.
Expanding vaccines was his foremost goal.
Those crucial efforts continue to unfold.
Nearly half of schools are open for learning,
The day for which many had been yearning.
Next was reviving our economy.
The Rescue Plan provides help to so many.
"I'm here to solve problems, not create divisions."
He's faced with numerous weighty decisions.
  Biden listened to "the press" intently,
  Addressing questions comprehensively.

3/26/2021

Other questions and responses involved infrastructure; immigration and the multitudes of unaccompanied minors at the border; gun control; voting rights and the filibuster; dealing with North Korea and recent ballistic missile testing; plans to leave Afghanistan and disentangle from foreign wars; holding China accountable through democracies working together; environmental challenges posed by global warming; rebuilding our inadequate highways, bridges, and airports; recapping wells leaking methane; repairing schools with lead in pipes, asbestos, and poor systems of ventilation; and research to defeat cancer, Alzheimer's and diabetes.

"We can't build back the way it used to be, due to global warming and environmental changes. But there is so much we can do to make people healthier and create good jobs. I can't guarantee we can solve everything, but we can make things better," President Biden concluded.

NATIVE AMERICAN CABINET SECRETARY

Deb Haaland of the Laguna Pueblo
Will be the first Native since years ago
To serve in a high U.S. government role.
Her job requirements will be manifold.
She will oversee lands and tribal nations,
Giving them reason for celebrations.
Haaland represents rich diversity,
Our first Native cabinet secretary.
"We must be good stewards of waters and land
And protect threatened species as best we can."
She'll review actions taken by Trump's teams
That allowed pollution of rivers and streams.
  She rejoices at the bald eagle's comeback.
  Banning DDT was an effective tack.

3/27/2021

The Laguna Pueblo is a 7,700 member tribe in west-central New Mexico. Haaland calls herself a 35th generation New Mexican, with roots she can trace there to the 1200s. She will oversee the Department of the Interior.

Haaland is the most senior Indigenous American in U.S. government since Republican Charles Curtis of the Kaw Nation served under Herbert Hoover as vice-president between 1929 and 1933.

Secretary Haaland will be tasked with overseeing and protecting U.S. public and tribal lands, while working to restore trust between the nation's 574 federally recognized tribes and the department that has often neglected them. The agency manages over 500 million acres of public land and houses the Bureau of Indian Affairs. She believes a balance is needed between protecting the environment and interests of fossil fuel industries.

RESTRAINT

Rochelle Walensky of the CDC
Made an emotional plea on TV.
Almost tearful, she confessed feeling "doom,"
That lethal variants could dominate soon.
"We may be *weeks* from regaining control,
But risky behaviors could inflict a toll."
She pleaded that we take precautions longer.
We *can* defeat COVID and emerge stronger.
The race is on – mutations or vaccine?
Another surge could be as bad as we've seen.
"Rejecting science got us where we are today."
Right actions *now* send COVID on its way.
  She put down her script and spoke from her heart.
  It's up to us now to do our own part.

3/30/2021

Dr. Rochelle Walensky is the Director of the Center for Disease Control (CDC), appointed by President Biden. Both she and the president made heartfelt appeals to show restraint in our plans and activities for six to eight more weeks, until larger numbers of our population are completely vaccinated. At this point, the majority – 85 percent – have NOT been given protections of an effective vaccine from Pfizer, Moderna or Johnson & Johnson.

We are making good progress – with up to 3 million being vaccinated a day – but new cases are rising across the land, and there will undoubtedly be a spike after spring break and Easter celebrations. If variants succeed in compromising the vaccines' effectiveness, our recovery will be greatly set back, and countless other lives may be needlessly lost.

LESSONS OF COVID-19

What have I learned in my introspection
This year of the dreaded COVID infection?
My home has become my sanctuary
Which I can secure if times turn scary.
I'm proud I've learned to be self-reliant
And when needed, I can be defiant.
I've multiple ways to remain content,
Steeped in reading or movies as time well spent.
I delight in my garden around me.
Wild birds and squirrels are a joy to see.
I've grown more patient and accept my plight.
I'm energized by the sonnets I write.
  One day I'll resume my busier life,
  But sometimes I'll miss my days of less strife.

3/30/2021

I have fortified my house against potential home invasions, but living here poses ever-present risks of major earthquakes, wildfires, and smoke-filled, hazardous air. My house is earthquake retrofitted and I have fire-retardant asphalt shingles on my roof. I removed all flammable vegetation such as juniper landscaping and cut down trees that formerly hung over my roof. I may eventually have to take out Monterrey pines at the back end of my property. Droughts cause stress to the towering trees, making them likely targets of bark beetles that kill them and increase fire danger. These are aspects of California living I must cope with, but I would not want to live anywhere else.

PART II – NEVER TRULY GONE

IN MEMORY

VICTOR ALBERT ROYER

September 23, 1936 – March 30, 2016

I would not be writing sonnets today if it weren't for Victor's appreciation for Shakespeare's sonnets. He often read and recited them from memory for me. I began to write in that format for his birthday and Valentine's Day.

As his death approached, I took comfort in composing sonnets to deal with my anguish and grief. I found a sonnet on his digital recorder as a parting message of love to me while he was in the final stages of pancreatic cancer.

I would never have attempted to write sonnets, or this book, if it hadn't been for Victor's influence and encouragement. He loved the sonnets that I wrote for him. He would say, "I don't know how you do it." Coming from a renaissance man like him, that was a great compliment.

Victor was an artist and Fulbright scholar who could do almost anything creative. He was an internationally recognized sculptor. A gifted teacher, he taught sculpture and art history at U.C. Berkeley and the University of Melbourne. His sculpture was featured in six one-man shows in San Francisco during the 1960s and 1970s. Victor also built a fortepiano, constructed a large telescope, and he recited sonnets beautifully. I enjoyed hearing him play Chopin and Mozart daily on his piano. If I was on the phone, I would often hear, "That's a beautiful CD."

My soul mate and beloved partner of twenty-three years died too soon, but he lives on in my heart.

GRIEF SUPPORT GROUP – HEALING WILL COME

After Victor's death from pancreatic cancer, I joined a grief support group for those who had recently lost a spouse. I shared my "Victor" sonnets. Group members seemed to relate to emotions I expressed. During this difficult time, when so many thousands have lost loved ones to COVID-19, I decided to include my bereavement sonnets.

As President Biden says to those who grieve: "The time will come when your loved one's memory will bring a smile to your lips before it brings a tear to your eye. I promise you."

It took me five years!

SONNETS OF LOVE AND LOSS

FOR VICTOR ROYER

Written 2014 - 2021

Victor at the five-octave fortepiano he built for his use. One of his small sculptures is in the foreground in his Oakland studio.

WILL YOU STILL LOVE ME?

The summer face you knew when we first met
Is now reflecting autumn's golden hue.
You tell me that my beauty lingers yet;
My mind and body still appeal to you.
But when my locks have changed to winter white,
My body weak or mind be clouded o'er,
And tho' my daily discourse may seem trite,
Will you still love me as you did before?
And should a curving spine decrease my height
Or cause my steps to falter on their way,
Would you still see my face with some delight
And tell me you are here with me to stay?
   And if, one day, I can't recall your name,
   Will your affection still remain the same?

2/6/2014

I read this poem in Berkeley for **Bay Area Generations**. That exciting poetry-reading series featured the paring of an older poet with another poet a generation younger than the first reader. Poems were curated, with readers selected by a volunteer panel. The series was also videotaped. It was an honor for me to be selected to read with that prestigious group of Bay Area poets.

LOVE IS AGELESS

To hear you speak such somber words of late
Brings fear and dread of our impending fate.
You lifted my battered body and soul
And with an artist's hands you made me whole.
I see you as my brilliant guiding star
And I am most contented where you are.
Your face, now fringed with beard of snowy white,
Gives comfort in first rays of morning light.
Though hands lose strength and gaits decrease in stride,
The wellspring of our youth remains inside.
I ask, do not decry our altered state.
I'll love you to the end, my cherished mate.
    Our eyes may dim, our passion may subside,
    But I will always want you by my side.

2/15/2015

WINTER APPROACHES

The sundrenched days of summer when we met
Are now for us a distant memory.
I feel a strong attraction to you yet.
Through twenty springs we've lived in harmony.
To spend each day with you is a delight
In sharing music, films and poetry.
But now your face appears in waning light,
And winter soon will claim our custody.
The speeding up of time intensifies
The love I feel and dread of losing you.
I see the warning signs of our demise.
We soon shall vanish like the morning dew.
    When rough winds shake the leaves from winter trees,
    The loss of you would bring me to my knees.

11/2/2015

Victor would often read or recite to me **Shakespeare's Sonnet 73**, as though warning me that his own end was near. The verse about "Bare ruin'd choirs, where late the sweet birds sang ..." always made me sad. He sensed changes taking place in his body, and he was trying to prepare me for the idea that one day soon, he must leave me alone. I wrote **"Winter Approaches"** for him in response. It was one of my earliest sonnets addressed to him. He was seventy-eight at the time.

"That time of year thou mayst in me behold
When yellow leaves, or none, or few, do hang
Upon those boughs which shake against the cold,
Bare ruin'd choirs, where late the sweet birds sang..."

CONSTANCY

How like a god you were when we first met.
Your muscled body gleamed so in the sun.
Since twenty years have passed, I see you yet
As one I'll cherish 'til our lives are done.
Although your health and strength have now declined,
Your fall and broken hip have brought dismay,
Your mind and spirit cannot be confined
Within these walls that now define your day.
I'll care for you with tender ministries
As you have done for me in my distress.
Our love cannot be dimmed by mere disease.
My life without you would be emptiness.
  The flame of love continues to burn bright.
  I'll be here when you need me, day or night.

1/15/2016

THE HARDEST TIME OF YEAR

The hardest time to lose you would be springtime
With new growth bursting in the air,
When birdsong sounds unspeakably sublime,
And bulbs and trees are flowering everywhere.
More difficult is summer for goodbyes
When early fog dissolves in sundrenched days.
The tears would often well up in my eyes.
I'd stumble as I wandered through a maze.
When fall arrives with leaves of red and gold
That let go gently, forming flaming piles,
How painful it would be to not behold
Your handsome face that radiates your smiles.
  In winter, could I bear to part with you?
  Not in those dreary days of somber hue!

2/29/16 (completed the day before Victor died)

I started writing this one while waiting for Victor to emerge from the Special Procedures Suite, where he was undergoing a process to unblock the bile duct tubes. This procedure, called an ERCP, normally took less than an hour. After four hours the doctor had to give up. Tumors were blocking the tubes. They discharged him to home with me in a pouring rain. He received no pain medication. A side-effect for 48 hours after general anesthesia can be depression. They didn't call him the next day.

After he died, I painstakingly documented his substandard care and filed complaints by going through the hospital ombudsman. I met with a panel, giving them a list of twelve suggestions for the improved coordination and support for patients diagnosed with terminal cancer. I believe I may have helped other patients.

NEW DAWN AFTER YOU

I start each day with loving thoughts of you.
I try to concentrate on things to do.
I miss the morning rituals we shared.
Around me are reminders how you cared.
I seem to measure time in different ways.
All nature now looks shrouded in thick haze,
And birdsong sounds too harsh and out of tune.
The first full moon without you will rise soon.
The longer springtime days once brought me cheer,
But I will not be comforted this year.
Somehow, I'll find the strength to carry on.
I'll cherish all you were, until I'm gone.
  How blessed we were to know love from the start.
  My love for you will always fill my heart.

4/19/2016

WITHOUT YOU HERE

To lose you in the spring was devastating.
Each morn I wake alone to greet the day.
I wish you had decided to keep waiting.
I know the reasons why you could not stay.
I miss your arms that held me close to you;
Your love for me I knew you'd not betray.
I need your strength for tasks I cannot do;
Your insights on the news that brings dismay.
Now that you're gone, the birds have ceased their singing.
The daytime skies have turned a leaden grey
And butterflies have lost their zest for winging,
The stars shine dimmer in the Milky Way.
  Too soon, that day I dreaded has come true.
  How hard it is to be here without you.

5/26/2016

POST-ELECTION HOLIDAZE

The longer nights and cold north winds are here,
The time of year that I would sometimes dread.
This season should be joyful, but I fear
The storm clouds I see threatening ahead.
If only you were here to see me through
The challenges of living out my life,
I'd face each day, content to be with you
While insulated from the looming strife.
This fall, it's strange to see the seasons clash –
With leaves aflame and tulip trees in bloom –
As nature out of synch reflects the flash
Of tempers in our nation, plunged in gloom.
  I'm sometimes glad you didn't live to see
  Our nation torn in such disharmony.

11/27/2016

Donald Trump was elected president as a result of the Electoral College totals, despite losing the popular vote to Hillary Clinton by more than three million votes. Protests sprang up immediately. Women's marches were especially prominent. A win for Hillary had been predicted, and women looked forward to having our first female president. The glass ceiling had been cracked, but it remained unbroken.

Victor and I were of the same mind about politics. He was a Democrat and he supported Hillary Clinton, as I did.

PAINFUL MEMORIES

My beauty vanished on the day you died.
The shock and grief are etched into my face.
My sleep is fitful since you left my side.
I wake without your comforting embrace.
I try to hold back tears and flash a smile,
But those who know me well can sense my pain,
That I am thinking of you all the while.
My sonnets always have a sad refrain.
Perhaps in spring my spirits will revive,
When daffodils are shining in the sun,
The way they gleamed when you were last alive.
I found you there among them with your gun.
  I wish that we had kissed and said, "Goodbye."
  You *could* have had a gentler way to die.

1/12/2017

I was told it would take *thirty days* to set up Home Hospice. Victor could not wait. He ended his life because of unremitting pain, with no access to drugs such as codeine or morphine.

Victor died on March 30, 2016, a few months before Death with Dignity (Assisted Dying) was implemented in California. The California Legislature had passed the *compassionate choices* measure, but funding for the medication had not yet been approved. Before receiving the oral drugs, the patient had to be of sound mind and able to administer the medication to himself. Approval of two physicians over a two-week period was required. A doctor must also be present at the end. A dear friend with cancer had a beautiful passage in 2020, utilizing the recent laws.

MY LOST VALENTINE

I missed you so today, my valentine,
As daffodils are blooming on our hill.
This time last year, your heart and soul were mine.
Today, I spoke as though you were here still.
If only you could whisper back to me
And tell me we will meet again one day.
The end of life is such a mystery.
There are so many things I'd want to say.
You left so soon, we didn't kiss goodbye.
You couldn't see the trauma you would cause.
Almost a year has passed, and yet I cry.
If you had known, it might have made you pause.
  Soon, I hope my grief will be diminished.
  Love for you will last till time is finished.

2/14/2017

I wrote this one before I fell asleep around midnight. That first Valentine's Day was the most difficult.

SPRING'S REMINDERS

I see early signs of spring coming on,
Almost three years since my love has been gone.
How cruel of nature to take him in spring,
A time of renewal when birds again sing.
We knew his days with me soon would be ending.
He tried to prepare me without offending.
I'd feared he would take his fate in his hands,
But it wasn't my place to make demands.
His gravest concern was to leave me alone.
He harbored no thought of sin to atone.
His cancer stole him away far too soon.
I miss him intensely on nights with full moon.
  As daffodils sway in the place where he lay,
  I remember Victor with love today.

2/26/2019

Although he ended his life while suffering from pancreatic cancer, in my mind, it was his terminal illness that killed him. I found him in our backyard, in a patch of spent daffodils – the flower celebrated by cancer survivors. Victor Royer, my beloved partner of twenty-three years, died in late March of 2016. The Hospice we requested had been delayed, and his pain was unbearable.

Victor's pancreatic cancer was not detected until he was close to death. As his time with me drew to a close, I took some comfort in writing sonnets to help relieve my stress and grief. The day he died, I found a sonnet by Shakespeare on his digital recorder as a parting message of love. I would never have attempted to write sonnets, or this book, if it hadn't been for Victor's love of reading and reciting sonnets and his encouragement when I dared to try the difficult format myself.

CALIFORNIA SPRINGTIME

Oh, the joy of spring with fragrance in the breeze
That caresses petals of budding fruit trees.
Poppies and daffodils bloom all around,
And soon blue iris will poke through the ground.
Mockingbirds tune up to attract a mate.
Emerald hummingbirds are migrating late.
In the springtime, thoughts may turn to romance,
But I lack a partner to join in that dance.
I have no desire to find someone new.
None would compare with the partner I knew.
In Victor I found true compatibility,
One who proved his strong devotion to me.
  I've had a sweetheart who made me feel cherished.
  The love I knew with him has not perished.

3/4/2021

Nearly five years since Victor died in late March of 2016, I have finally arrived at a point where I can appreciate spring again.

Many of my poems mention birds. We were both avid bird watchers. Victor built a platform outside our bedroom window where a great variety of birds came each day for wild bird seed. I now have *two* hummingbird feeders, with so many visitors this time of year that I must replenish the sugar water once a day.

I was thrilled to find mockingbirds, the state bird of Texas, in this neighborhood. They are a delight in late spring and summer, as are the robins calling to each other with their lovely, lilting songs.

A VISION OF BEAUTY

March 30th this year was a better day.
It marked five years since Victor passed away.
The morning started with a novel scene
That left me breathless, but feeling serene.
I awoke before six and opened the drape,
Surprised by a wondrous scene taking shape.
The setting full moon hung over my hill
Framed perfectly by pines in morning's chill.
It felt like a message from Victor to me
That he waits for me in eternity.
He seemed to be sharing again our delight,
As on many a cloudless, full moon night.
  I had missed the moonrise the night before.
  What a lovely treat Victor had in store.

3/31/2021

I was immediately comforted by this lovely vision. Within two minutes the moon had dipped below the hill, but I felt at peace all day on that awful anniversary. I believe that I am now finally past the worst of my grief.

Victor loved to look at the heavens before retiring each night. He knew astronomy and for decades had studied the skies with the powerful 8-inch, reflecting telescope he made. We were able to see the moons of Jupiter and rings of Saturn through it.

Whenever weather conditions were good for viewing, we had a ritual of going up the hill to watch the full moon coming up over the ridge at the horse stables.

THE WAY WE WERE – VICTOR AND ANNA

In the springtime of our love, March 1994

I brought my love some daffodils
To brighten up her day.
"But, oh my dear, my allergies."
I hastened them away.

By Victor Royer

Victor had a great sense of humor. I was allergic to the pollen-laden daffodils that he brought indoors for our table. Roses and iris were fine, but he learned to leave the daffodils blooming outdoors.

LOVE SONNET FOR ANNA

I never gave my love a Valentine,
although in every other thing I did
I was attentive to her every need,
and called her Queen, and Mistress of my Soul.

But she was somehow strangely discontent,
and told me so in words of simple force:
that my account of love was in arrears
because I never wrote a single word.

My spoken word was adequate for me
to say the things I wanted her to hear:
but she would have me write my words of praise,
immortalized for her in blackest ink.

And so I write, and so do I declare:
That Anna Henny is beyond compare.

Victor Royer
March 6, 2015

I conclude my book with this beautiful sonnet that Victor wrote for me about a year before he died. This poem is further proof that Victor could accomplish almost anything creative that he set his mind to do. He DID give me valentines sometimes, but I didn't need those as proof of his love. He demonstrated his devotion to me every day of our lives together. I might add that this sonnet uses iambic pentameter perfectly.

PART III – APPENDIX

ACKNOWLEDGMENTS

The comments and enthusiasm of family members and close friends led me to believe that my poems might provide a valuable historical perspective. They encouraged me to share my writing with a wider audience. I am grateful to all who gave feedback and who looked forward to receiving my **poetic news flashes**. I especially appreciate the time and efforts of Jean Gregory and Susan ten Bosch Paull, who read my poems, gave me excellent suggestions and wrote reviews for my book.

Others who encouraged me to publish were my cousins Kay Past, Pat Henny, and Evelyn Malone, LMFT, as well as my daughter, Dr. Karen Dabney-Lieras, my son Rob Dabney and wife Dr. Karla Robleto, and good friends Debbie Andrews and Babs Callaway.

I also owe a huge debt of gratitude to friends in my writers' group, formed by brilliant poetry and prose writer Margaret Irvin. She has capably led our group for over two decades. I appreciate all the members who listened and reacted to my poems in this collection. Additional persons lending strong support to my efforts were multi-talented writer and performer Melinda Maxwell-Smith, published novelist Jan Stites and gifted poet Gail Onion, who helped me to refine my book's title.

Throughout this "year of the plague," the empathy, concern and caring of my fellow writers helped me to persevere in my isolation. I would never have embarked on my publishing journey without them cheering for me every step along the way.

Additionally, I want to recognize Patricia Pillard McCulley and Byron McCulley, publishing consultants for Interdimensional Press, who assisted me in the publishing process. An author of several books, Patricia was a great help with her sharp eye for detail. Byron was able to conceptualize and create the cover designs that I suggested to him, with exciting results.

ABOUT THE AUTHOR

Anna Henny Dabney grew up in Texas with an irrepressible desire to see the world. After graduating from the University of North Texas, she taught English and music in Dallas before accepting a job with the Air Force to teach American dependents. She lived overseas for three years, teaching in Turkey, Germany and France. Married in Europe to U.S. civilian Bob Dabney, she and her husband enjoyed extensive travel before returning to the United States.

Anna is the daughter of a Dutch immigrant who arrived in the northern U.S. in his late teens and who became successful in business. Work took him to South Texas, where he remained the rest of his life. In 1918, Carl Henny volunteered for hazardous duty during World War I, serving in Eastern France in directing the demolition of artillery shells in the fields near Metz. Anna and Bob would live in that same area many years later.

Anna's world view was greatly influenced by her cultured and tolerant father who in his youth loved to travel. He was a patriot, flying our flag on special days and keeping up with current affairs in the U.S. and around the world. Her mother trusted his opinions and always voted the same way he did. The daughter of a cattleman and rancher, she was the family's spiritual leader.

Leaving France in 1966, Anna and Bob soon found good jobs in the California Bay Area. Anna taught English until their second child was born. With both children in school, she changed careers, serving as director of public relations at two Bay Area hospitals. She earned her accreditation in public relations (APR) from the Public Relations Society of America. In the mid-1990s, she formed her own business, *AD Communications,* working as a writing consultant for various Bay Area hospitals and health systems. After the births of grandchildren William and Mia, Anna published two photo books with her poems about wildlife: ***Come to the Zoo – Photos & Haiku*** (2013) and ***The Rhyme & Reason of Wildlife (2014)***. Both books display full-page color photos – with over half of them taken herself. The second book won a "Moonbeam" Award in international competition in 2015.

Anna is primarily a prose writer, but she has written poetry for three decades. She has presented poems from her award-winning poetry chapbook, ***Life after Breast Cancer***, for the Susan G. Komen Foundation and Kaiser Permanente's forum on cancer. In addition, she performed her poems for Bay Area Generations and for various open mics.

The Oakland resident is a long-standing participant with a writers' group affiliated with Montclair Presbyterian Church. Anna is extremely grateful for the inspiration, encouragement and deep friendships which the group provides. Meetings and open mics now take place virtually using Zoom and help to ease feelings of isolation during these challenging times.

(Author Photo by poet Barb Reynolds)

SERENDIPITY!

Around 1978, Joe Biden attended a banquet hosted by Laney College's Culinary Arts Program in Oakland, California. I was assigned to photograph him for the *Laney Tower* newspaper. After nine years of teaching English, and with both children in school, I enrolled in community college to study journalism. I intended to transition into public relations work.

Joe Biden was engaging and genuine, asking me about myself and my interests. I have never forgotten that happy exchange. I never dreamed I was photographing a future U.S. president.

I developed the film and printed this photo in my darkroom. Years later, I scanned and converted to digital format my portrait of Joe Biden. I treasure it!

Photo by Anna Henny Dabney

REVIEWS for Pandemic and Politics Poems...

"Anna's views on pandemic and politics are set like jewels in the shimmering settings of her sonnets. Her voice is at once tender and urgent. Amidst the chaos of the past year, the consistency of the sonnet form is a comforting way to receive her 'poetic news flashes.' Reading one leads to another and another and another. Like fine chocolate. Soothing to the soul."

–Melinda Maxwell-Smith, MT, RCST, SEP, Trauma Specialist

"Anna Dabney writes with enormous empathy as she documents daily griefs and barrages endured by many who became heart-sore and weary during a year of almost unbelievable intensity. Anna's beautifully crafted sonnets and prose, sure to resonate with readers, give voice to days of enormous despair – but also to moments of joy and magic. Treat yourself to this remarkable collection."

–Jan Stites, author of *Edgewise* and *Reading the Sweet Oak*

"Anna Dabney is the only person I know of who described the pandemic and politics of 2020 – 2021 poetically. Year of the Plague Journal *is an amazing collection of her beautifully worded sonnets, dealing with everything from the coronavirus to George Floyd's tragic death, Ruth Bader Ginsburg's passing, Biden's victory, the January 6th insurrection—and even one honoring Dr. Jennifer Doudna for her Nobel Prize work in CRISPR gene editing. I can't imagine a better 'history' of the plague year than this creative one."*

–Kay Past, retired Spanish teacher, columnist, family historian

REVIEWS for Love and Loss Poems...

"In her 'love and loss' sonnets for Victor, Anna creates such beauty and truth from the unbearable pain. She speaks for so many who have suffered loss, helping them to cope, and giving them comfort that someone else knows their suffering, too."

–Jean Gregory, Oakland writer and performance artist

"Anna's grief sonnets represent so completely the love she and Victor shared, their journey as he battled late-stage pancreatic cancer, and her brave recovery over time. People will marvel at the deep love and strong connection between the two of them and Anna's talent in expressing it. All of her heartfelt poems will resonate with readers on many levels."

–Susan ten Bosch Paull, dear friend of Anna and Victor